WRITING
IS
EXCITING

Guided Writing Lessons for 3rd Grade

Written by Julie Coan

© 2011 Julie Coan
www.WritingandKids.com
Far Journeys Books 1105 N. Chapel Hill Ave. Clovis, CA 93611
Email: WritingBooksIsEasy@hotmail.com
ISBN: 978-0615556406
Cover image licensed by Depositphotos.com/Monkey business
Printed in the United States of America

Table of Contents

INTRODUCTION

What is Guided Writing?

Students can't learn to write well by being assigned random, unstructured writing assignments. Writing skills must be taught in a sequential manner with built-in practice and periodic review. Each skill must be effectively modeled and students must be supported as they learn. I call this process *Guided Writing*.

Better Writers Make Better Readers

Reading alone will only take students to a certain level of comprehension. If children are to truly understand what they read, then they must be writers as well as readers. We want students to understand not just the words, but the rhythms and the strategies that create power in our written words. By writing things that others can read, they are practicing in intimate detail the creation of readable material. By experiencing this, they can better understand what others have written.

How can this book help you?

First, and most importantly, this book is designed to help make teaching writing easy, fun, and highly effective. Your colleagues will wonder what tricks you used to teach your students to write so well.

This book seeks to provide teachers with a road map for a child's first experiences with real writing. In third grade, students transition from learning to read to reading to learn. Along with this transition, students also transition into their first structured independent writing. They move beyond the initial structure of sentences into the more complex structures of paragraphs and beyond. So this book would ideally be used for students in the third grade. However, if the students have not learned these techniques in previous years, this book can be used in fourth or even fifth grade.

This book provides a comprehensive, sequential set of writing lessons. You won't have to worry about what writing skill should come next or figuring out the best way to teach paragraph writing. It's all laid out for you like a road map.

This book will show you:

- …how to create a writer-friendly environment in 10 easy steps.
- …how to teach your students to write such awesome descriptions that your colleagues will wonder how you did it.
- …how to teach your students to write stories you actually want to read.
- …how to get students to write a correctly structured paragraph every single time.
- …the simplest way to help students revise their writing.
- …the most effective way to teach students how to respond to literature.

THE FLEX CALENDAR

Whether you love to teach writing or it's only an afterthought in your classroom, this book will help mould your writing program into a powerful component of your curriculum. One of the unique strengths of this book is that the lessons are arranged sequentially for you. You don't have to think about which lesson to teach first. It's all mapped out for you with an easy to use flex calendar.

Follow the Calendar

The lessons in this book are arranged by topic so that you can easily see the progression of skills within each topic. However, the lessons aren't meant to be taught in order from the beginning of the book to the end of the book. Instead, the lesson order is laid out in the flex calendar.

The flex calendar is designed to help set a pace for the instruction and insure a balance of new instruction, continued review, and scaffolded practice. The lessons are designed to begin with highly-modeled activities and gradually progress until students are able to complete the activities independently.

The flex calendar is called the flex calendar because it is flexible. It allows time for you to spend more, or less time on an activity based on the needs of your students. It's important to follow the lessons in the order they appear on the calendar. Don't skip lessons or do them in a different order.

Track Your Progress

You'll want to use the calendar to track your progress. Check off each lesson as you complete it. If you need more days than are scheduled, simply continue to work on the lesson until you're finished, and then proceed to the next lesson. If you use fewer days than allotted, simply check off the remaining days and move to the next lesson.

You can simply copy the calendar provided in this book and check off each lesson with a pen. You can also download the pdf version from the website to your computer. It comes with check boxes that you simply click on as you finish each lesson.

WEB SUPPORT

This book is web-supported. We want this book to be as easy to use as possible so we've added materials that you can access online. Our website is www.WritingandKids.com.

You can…

- download the demonstration pages to your computer for use on your smart board.
- download the flex calendar.
- find Power Point presentations and videos for selected lessons.
- watch demonstration videos.
- look at samples of actual student work.
- visit our blog and ask questions.
- suggest improvements or new lesson ideas.
- get discounts and free materials.
- find recommended teacher materials. Do you waste money on teacher materials you never use? Find a list of the materials teachers have tried and labeled as "must-haves".

MAKING TIME FOR WRITING

Sometimes it's difficult to find time for writing when there seem to be so many other things to fit into your schedule. Writing time does not always have to be a separate activity. It can be part of your language arts block, but you can also incorporate writing lessons in your science or social studies lessons. Students will actually learn the material being taught in those subjects faster and easier if they use the writing techniques described in this book.

Write Every Day

The school year should begin with guided writing lessons only. After the first several weeks, independent writing lessons should be added. Every day, students should be given an independent writing assignment and a guided writing lesson. Although this book is focused on guided writing, some basic guidelines regarding independent writing are also included.

THE WRITING PROCESS

The lessons in the book follow the standard writing process. Students must internalize the writing process in order to become good writers. To do that, they must be taught the process and they must practice it over and over.

When professional writers write, their goal is to get their work published. They will use all five processes for every project, and they may repeat the revising and editing processes multiple times.

While most teachers agree that this is a valuable process, most will also agree that there is not enough time in a school year to go through every step of the writing process with every single writing project.

All writing has value. The act of practicing writing is important, even if no one ever reads it or grades it. Therefore, some of the lessons in this book will complete the entire process while some will only complete part of the process.

For those of you that are unfamiliar with the writing process, the steps are listed here.

Step One: Pre-write

Every writing assignment should start with this step. This step is designed to get students' brains activated. It may involve reading a book or portion of a book to them, brainstorming, or using a graphic organizer.

Step Two: Rough Draft

This is the step where students actually write the first draft of their composition. The rough draft should be written as quickly as possible. The focus should be on ideas and not form or conventions.

Step Three: Revise

During this step students will review their writing and find ways to make it better. Here's where they will organize ideas, move sentences and paragraphs, and cross out superfluous chatter.

Step Four: Edit

The editing phase is primarily used to fix writing conventions and spelling.

Step Five: Final Copy and Publishing

The final step of the writing process allows students to create a final, neat copy and publish it.

CREATING A WRITER-FRIENDLY ENVIRONMENT IN THE CLASSROOM...

One of the most important ingredients of a successful writing program is creating and maintaining a positive atmosphere in the classroom. This may mean changing or letting go of some of the more traditional ideas about teaching writing. It means thinking more like a writer and less like a teacher. Here are ten important aphorisms that writers know about writing.

1. Writing is messy.

Unlike nice tidy worksheets, all the answers will not look the same. Not all students will take the same amount of time or write the same amount. Students can cross things out, draw big arrows to move things to other places, and write in the margins.

2. Writing is a team sport.

Traditionally, there has been a big emphasis on letting the student write without teacher assistance. Yet, in the real world, every book on the bookshelf has been changed and contributed-to by numerous editors, readers, and marketing specialists before it was published.

Although the original idea and the writing itself should be the child's, it's okay to suggest ideas to add to the story or ways to change a sentence or paragraph that will make the writing better. The teacher and the child become partners in the writing process.

3. It's okay to teach students to write according to a format.

Ninety percent of all professional writers write their books and stories using the same formats presented in this book. Writing with a format won't stifle students' creativity. In fact, the format provides a feeling of safety. Students won't sit and stare at their paper and search for a starting place.

4. Whatever students write, it can't be wrong!

The goal is to empower students. Putting letter grades on students' writing papers and covering them with red ink corrections sends the message that they are not good writers. The result is that they will be afraid to take chances with their writing and it is through taking those chances that students grow to be better writers.

5. Always provide a prompt or pre-writing activity.

Writing does not happen in a vacuum. Students' brains need to be engaged in the subject before they can write. Teachers that hand students a piece of paper and say, "Write a story. You have half an hour," will have a classroom full of students who hate to write.

6. Length does not always equal quality.

One student may write an absolutely stunning composition that is only two paragraphs long. That composition may be much better than another student's writing that is two pages long. It's okay to set target lengths for assignments and even to encourage students to write more. The correct answer to "How much do I have to write?"is, "Until you are finished."

7. Sometimes it's okay to write garbage.

Expecting perfection in a single draft is not realistic, and it's not conducive to the production of quality writing. Imagine that you have to write an essay about teaching in order to keep your job. Would you write it and turn in the first draft? If a student thinks they have to write something perfectly the first time out, they will sit and stare at the blank piece of paper and nothing will ever get written.

Trying to formulate the perfect sentence or paragraph or scene before writing it is the number one cause of writers' block (for both children and adults). It is a fact that the act of moving the pencil on the paper actually starts the brain thinking. Many published writers will either copy from a printed book or copy something they have already written until the new words and ideas take over. Give your students permission to write garbage.

8. Every student's ideas are unique.

Every child's brain is unique. Their experiences are unique. They are capable of thinking thoughts that no one has thought before. It is important that this message is shared with students over and over again. Praise their writing. Celebrate their wonderful ideas. Make them believe the message.

9. Spelling can wait.

Spelling is important and correct spelling should be encouraged. It is important to explain to students that the reason they are writing is so that they can share their ideas with other people. If their spelling is so bad that the person who is reading their work can't understand what they have written, then they have wasted their time.

However, when students are writing rough drafts, getting good ideas down onto the paper must be the priority. If a teacher requires correct spelling during the rough draft, the final piece of writing will not be the student's best effort. When a child must stop and look up a word in a dictionary or ask someone how to spell a word, they lose their train of thought and their writing momentum will slow to a standstill.

Spelling is easy enough to correct during the editing phase. Students' spelling will improve throughout the year with a prolific amount of reading and writing and nothing else. Specific ways to improve spelling are covered under the editing addendum at the back of this book.

10. Celebrate every word.

Praise students for their efforts. Be amazed at their word choices. Share great tidbits with the class at random times. Let students know that their words are important and that their ideas count. Tell them often that they are great writers. Post their published works with flair.

Keep the first few writing assignments from the beginning of the year and then keep a few representative samples throughout the year. It is important for students to self-evaluate the progress of their writing skills. One of the best ways for them to do that is to look back periodically at those first pieces of writing. Students are always amazed at how much they have grown as writers.

White Boards

In the "direct instruction" step, many lessons call for the use of individual white boards. If you don't have individual white boards for your students, you can substitute a clear page protector with a blank sheet of white paper inserted. Students can write with dry-erase pens or crayons and erase with a paper towel.

CONCEPT #1: FICTION AND NON-FICTION

Stop! If you are reading this section and you haven't read the previous section regarding the Flex Calendar, please go back and read it before proceeding. The lessons in this book aren't meant to be taught in numerical order.

Foundation Information

Once students become fluent readers, literary analysis will facilitate the learning of nearly everything else. Literary analysis is the process of evaluating the style and organization of written material. If students are to write well, they must first understand the different ways in which written material can be organized.

All written works can be divided into two categories: fiction and non-fiction. If students are to write well and comprehend what they read, they must first learn to distinguish between these two kinds of writing. Fiction and non-fiction works are written and read in two completely different ways. If they cannot recognize the difference, they will not know how the work is organized. The patterns that they use when they write will help them to see and understand the patterns in the books that they read. This, of course, facilitates comprehension and retention.

What is the difference between fiction and non-fiction writing?

The primary distinction comes from the content of the writing. By definition, fiction is writing that comes from the imagination. Non-fiction is writing about things that are real.

The most important difference, though, is in the structure. Fiction is generally written from beginning to end. There is a distinct and recognizable beginning, middle, and end. This is why fiction stories should never be planned or analyzed using a web. A web goes out in all directions equally without a distinct starting and ending point. Non-fiction, with the possible exception of biographies, does not need to be written from beginning to end. I can pick up a non-fiction book and start on a chapter in the middle and understand what is going on. This is why a web is an excellent tool for planning non-fiction writing.

Fiction/Non-fiction Key Teaching Points

Fiction

1. written from imagination

2. written and read from beginning to end (one direction)

3. read for enjoyment

Non-fiction

1. real

2. may be written or read in any direction

3. read to get information

Whenever a new lesson is introduced during the year, students should be asked these three essential questions:

1. Is this a work of fiction or non-fiction?

2. How do you know? (Answers should match those items above.)

3. Why is it important to know this?

I will know how the book is organized.

I will know how to read it.

Lesson #1: Fiction-Non-Fiction

Step One: Direct Instruction

Introduce the key teaching points of fiction-non-fiction.

Step Two: Gather a selection of ten or twelve fiction and non-fiction books for every four students in your class. Textbooks are okay, but be sure to include some non-fiction selections that are not so obvious.

Divide students into groups of four. Give each group of students a set of books. Ask them to look at the titles and the tables of contents. Ask them to flip through the books. Working as a group, students will divide them into two stacks-- one for fiction and one for non-fiction.

Choose two students from each group. Choose a fiction and a non-fiction book and ask them to tell why they put each book into its category.

Step Three: Distribute Introduction to Fiction/Non-Fiction Worksheet #1 (p. 13) and clarify directions. Students should be able to complete the worksheet independently.

Lesson #2: Fiction-Non-fiction Card Game

Step One: Review

Correct the Introduction to Fiction/Non-Fiction Worksheet #1 and discuss mistakes. Review key teaching points. A In lieu of step one, you may use the Powerpoint presentation which is available online.

Step Two: Guided Practice

Distribute one FICTION card and

one NON-FICTION card to each student (p. 15).

Read the following titles one at a time. Wait five to ten seconds to give students "thinking time" and then give students a signal (i.e. snapping fingers or saying "Show me!"). Ask students to be silent until the signal. At the signal, students hold up the card that shows whether the title is non-fiction or fiction.

Ask the students, "How do you know?" Randomly choose two students to answer. Give the team a point for each correct answer.

Titles

1. All about Animals (Non-fiction)

2. How is Bread Made? (Non-fiction)

3. Gus the Grasshopper Goes to School (Fiction)

4. School Bus Rules (Non-fiction)

5. The Elephant Who Lived in a Shoe (Fiction)

6. The Martian's Vacation (Fiction)

7. Mary's Pet Hamster (Non-fiction)

8. How to Take Care of Your Pets (Non-fiction)

9. Computers are Easy (Non-fiction)

10. How to Turn Your Brother into a Frog (Fiction)

11. John's Spaceship Goes to Venus (Fiction)

12. The Giant Squid that Ate New York (Fiction)

13. The History of San Francisco (Non-fiction)

14. Earthquakes (Non-fiction)

15. The Owl's Dance (Fiction)

Step Three: Independent Practice

Distribute Fiction/Non-Fiction Practice #2 Worksheet (p. 14) and clarify directions.

Lesson #3: Characteristics of Fiction-Non-Fiction Activity

Step One: Preparation

Make one copy of Fiction/Non-Fiction Activity page (p. 16) for every three students. Cut the pages into three sections along the lines. This will give you enough cards to play the game three times.

Step Two: Review

Correct Fiction/Non-fiction Worksheet #2.

Step Three: Direct Instruction

Ask students to turn their worksheet to the back (which should be blank). Ask them to draw a line down the middle. Label one half FICTION and the other half NON-FICTION. Students should write down as many characteristics of fiction and non-fiction books as they can remember.

After 4-5 minutes, ask for volunteers to share one thing that they know. List them on the board under FICTION and NON-FICTION.

Fiction:

1. written from imagination

2. written from beginning to end

3. read for enjoyment

Non-fiction:

1. real

2. may be written or read in any direction

3. read to get information

Step Four: Guided Practice

Divide the class into groups of three to play the fiction/non-fiction game. Make sure everyone has a pencil.

Rules

Distribute one game card to each group of three.

When the teacher says START, the person with the paper in their possession will write fiction or non-fiction next to number one.

After ten seconds, the teacher will say "PASS". At that time, the person will

pass the paper to the next person who will write fiction or non-fiction next to #2.

Repeat this process until all the blanks are filled. For the first round only, leave the information on the board, so that students can refer to it for their answers.

Step Five: Review the answers together as a class. The group with the most correct answers is the winner.

Step Six: Erase the board. Play two more rounds.

Step Seven: Closure

Once again, ask the students to turn their paper to the blank side. Ask them to draw and line down the middle and label the sides "fiction" and "non-fiction". On the correct side, ask them to write down the three characteristics of each one.

Introduction to Fiction and Non-Fiction #1

Name _____

A. Directions: Write each item from the right under the correct title on the left.

FICTION

1._____

2._____

3._____

NON-FICTION

1._____

2._____

3._____

- Real
- Read from beginning to end
- Read for enjoyment
- Not real
- Read in any direction
- Read to get information

B. Directions: Read the following book titles and answer the questions below.

The title of a book is The Monkey's First Day of School.

1. Is this book fiction or non- fiction?_____

2. How do you know? _____

3. Why is it important to know this? _____

The title of a book is The Big Book of Birds.

4. Is this book fiction or non-fiction? _____

5. How do you know?_____

6. Why is it.important to know this? _____

C. Answer the following questions by writing "fiction" or "non- fiction" on the line.

7. Tracy is reading chapter 5 of her book first and then she will read chapter 8. Is her book fiction or non-fiction?_____

8. Matthew is spending his Saturday afternoon reading The Pirate's Gold. Is his book fiction or non-fiction? _____

9. Marissa needed to find out how much the Liberty Bell weighed so she looked in the book called The Beginning of the United States. Is her book fiction or non-fiction?

_____

10. Jason is reading How to Win Every Video Game Ever Made. Is his book fiction or non-fiction? _____

Fiction and Non-Fiction Practice #2

Name _____

A. Directions: Write fiction or non-fiction after each of these titles.

1. All About Birds   6. Alligators

2. Mrs. Mouse's Song   7. Flying Pigs

3. Jerry's Vacation   8. Monsters in my Desk

4. Ghosts in the Closet   9. Cake Recipes

5. Moon Rocks   10. Singing Raccoons

B. Directions: Write the titles of three fiction books. Don't forget to underline the important words in the title.

11. _____

12. _____

13. _____

Name three reasons why these books are fiction.

14. _____

15. _____

16. _____

C. Directions: Write the titles of three non-fiction books. Don't forget to underline the important words in the title.

17. _____

18. _____

19. _____

Tell three reasons why these books are non-fiction.

20. _____

21. _____

22. _____

fiction	non-fiction
fiction	non-fiction
fiction	non-fiction
fiction	non-fiction

Fiction/ Non-Fiction Activity: Round One

1. Real_____
2.   Pre-write using a web_____
3. Uses imagination_____
4. Read to get information_____
5. Read from beginning to end _____
6. Pre-write using characters, setting, plot _____
7. Can be read in any direction_____
8. Read mostly for enjoyment _____

Fiction/ Non-Fiction Activity: Round Two

1. Can be read in any direction _____
2.   Pre-write using characters, setting, plot _____
3.   Pre-write using a web_____
4. Read mostly for enjoyment _____
5. Read from beginning to end _____
6. Uses imagination_____
7. Read to get information_____
8. Real_____

Fiction/ Non-Fiction Activity: Round Three

1. Uses imagination_____
2. Read mostly for enjoyment _____
3. Real_____
4. Read from beginning to end _____
5. Pre-write using a web_____
6. Pre-write using characters, setting, plot _____
7. Can be read in any direction _____
8. Read to get information_____

CONCEPT #2: DESCRIPTIVE WRITING

Foundation Information

Description is a tool that is used in both fiction and non-fiction writing. Teaching students to describe things well is incredibly important. It makes the difference between writing that is mundane and writing that is exciting to read. We use descriptive writing to describe three things: people, places, and objects. The description of people will be covered in the section titled Characters. The description of places will be covered in the section titled Setting.

This section will only cover the description of objects. When a person is describing an object, they are attempting to change the way the reader views the object. They try to make the reader think about the object in a way they have never thought about it before.

Descriptive Writing Key Teaching Points

When writing description,

A. Write about each of the five senses

B. Describe how it makes you feel

C. Use a simile

Lesson #4:   Introduction to Object Description

Step One: Use direct instruction to teach the key teaching points of descriptive writing. A video is available online for this step.

Step Two: Pre-write

Place a small piece of chocolate or apple on a piece of paper towel on each student's desk. Popsicles, raisins, cereal, or cookies also work well. Distribute a copy of the Object Description Guide worksheet (p. 24) to help students stay focused. Begin by asking students to answer the two questions at the top of the page.

Ask students to just look at the object closely first. You may even want to provide magnifying glasses.   In the first square on their paper, ask them to write two words that tell how it looks. Next, ask them to use similes to compare the object to completely different object and write their sentence in the same square. Finally, students should write a sentence that tells what the object makes them think of. This can be a memory of an event or a person or a place.

Remind them that if the goal of their writing is positive, that is, if their goal is to show someone how good it is, they must use positive similes. If their goal is to show how awful something is, they should use similes that have a negative feel. It doesn't matter which one they choose, as long as they are consistent throughout the whole exercise. For example, if the student wants to tell about how wonderful a piece of chocolate is, they should not describe it as looking like doggie doo or a mud pie. They should describe it as a piece of happiness or a brown rainbow.

Repeat this process by smelling, touching, listening, and finally tasting the food sample. In the last square, students will write about how they feel inside.

Step Three: Rough Draft

Students will now write the information they have gathered onto a piece of lined paper. They should write in complete sentences. They should feel free to add, change, or take things out. The less sophisticated writers will write it exactly as it is on the guide sheet, changing nothing.

Step Four: Edit

Work with students in small groups to revise or eliminate sentences that are not as good as others. Keep only the best sentences.

Step Five: Final Draft

Students will write a final draft.

Step Six: Choose a Title

Students should choose a title for their piece. (See p. 133.)

Step Seven: Illustrate

Students may draw a picture to accompany their writing.

Step Eight: Publish

Students may publish their writing. Find five ways to publish students' work on p. 133.

Lesson #5: Object Description

Step One: Direct Instruction

Review the key teaching points for describing an object (or anything else). Make sure that students have a copy of the Descriptive Writing Chart #2 (p.57). Review the writing pattern shown on the Chart.

Step Two: Rough Draft

Choose an object for students to describe. It's best if it can be something that students can actually touch. The teacher can choose a common object from the classroom like a box of crayons or a pencil. They may also choose a common object from home like a candle, a paintbrush, or a measuring tape. Place the object where students can observe it.

Distribute lined paper and ask students to describe the object. They may refer to the Descriptive Writing Chart if they need to. The students' goal should be to write approximately half a page.

Step Three: Revise to Focus

When the object description is used as an independent piece of writing, it needs to contain its own focus. Because this technique is used for all independent forms of composition, it is described on p. 130.

Step Four: Revise Sentence Structure

In this step, students will revise the sentence structure in their description.

When students first learn to describe the setting, nearly all their sentences with begin with the word "I". A full page of writing should contain only five or six sentences that begin with "I". All the rest should be changed.

Step Five: Edit

Edit with students for spelling and grammar mistakes. Read about Editing on p. 132.

Step Six: Final Draft

Students will write a final draft.

Step Seven: Choose a Title

Students should choose a title for their piece. (See p. 133)

Step Eight: Illustrate

Students may draw a picture to accompany their writing.

Step Nine: Publish

Students may publish their writing. Read about five ways to publish students' work on p. 134.

Introduction to Similes

Foundation Information

It is important that students learn to use similes when they write. Like learning a new language, the earlier they learn to use it, the easier it is. Students at the third grade level can write wonderful similes once they learn how. It will soon become second nature to them. It isn't important at this stage that students are able to identify similes by name, but it is important that they become comfortable with their use and that they appreciate how much depth they can add to their writing.

Lesson #6: Introduction to Similes

Step One: Direct Instruction

Write **"The man was as tall as"** on the board. Ask students to supply a list of tall things to compare the man to. (It cannot be other people. The comparison must be between two <u>unlike</u> objects.)

Write **"The wind was as cold as"** on the board. Go around the room, making sure each child gives a response. Try to get them to expand on one-word responses. For example, if the child says "The wind was as cold as ice", ask where that ice is. Their new answers will be

"The wind was as cold as the ice on an iceberg" or "The wind was as cold as the ice at the North Pole".

Step Two: Guided Practice

On a piece of scratch paper, ask students to use a simile to finish this sentence. **The ant bite stung like...** Remind students they cannot compare this to another animal bite. Prompt them to think about other things that sting. When students are finished, share responses. Prompt students with one-word answers to add more information to it.

Example:

Good: The ant bite stung like a paper cut.

Better: The ant bite stung like sweat in a paper cut.

Repeat this process using these sentences:

The baby crawled on the floor like...

The marbles were round like...

The soccer ball flew across the field like...

Step Three: Students should choose their best sentence and write it at the bottom of a piece of unlined paper. They may then illustrate it.

Lesson #7: Similes--Practice Level 1

Step One: Direct Instruction

Teach the definition of a simile. "A simile is a comparison between two unlike objects using like or as." You may use the similes PowerPoint available online.

Step Two: Guided Practice

Distribute the worksheet Simile Practice #1 (p. 25). Use Sentences #1-5 to work with students. Allow students to share after each sentence. As you monitor, encourage them to lengthen and improve their sentences.

Step Three: Independent Practice

Students will complete Sentences #6-10 of Simile Practice #1 independently. If you wish, you can offer stickers or other small rewards for the best writing.

Lesson#8: Similes--Practice Level 2

Step One: Direct Instruction

Review the definition of a simile. Write this example on the board:

**My dog is as smart as
_____.**

Ask students to finish the sentence. Share answers.

Identify students that may need extra help during independent Practice.

Step Two: Guided Practice

Distribute the worksheet Simile Practice #2 (p. 26). Use sentences #1 and 2 as guided practice.   Identify any students that may still need individual help and work with them while the others are completing the independent practice.

Step Three: Independent Practice

Students will complete the remainder of the worksheet independently.

After completion, ask each child to choose their favorite simile. Publish it by printing it at the bottom of a piece of paper or letting the students write it themselves on the bottom of a piece of unlined paper. Students may illustrate and should be given time to share with the class.

Lesson #9: Settings Overloaded with Similes

Step One: Direct Instruction

Review descriptive writing and similes. Explain that today's exercise is meant to overload their writing with similes. Students need to understand that their final draft should never be overloaded with similes because it's too much for the reader to think about.

Instead of understanding something better, overloading will leave the reader confused. The purpose of this "overload" method is to help students find some unique and unusual ideas.

Step Two: Guided Practice

Distribute lined paper. Use the Simile Overload demonstration page (p. 52). Point out that the first three sentences tell about things that can be seen. The items that were chosen are small details. All the details the students choose should be small details. Highlight the simile following each "sense" sentence.

Ask students to close their eyes and imagine themselves in a movie theater. Ask them to write a sentence about something they see. Then write a simile. Ask them to share with a partner and then ask for a few random volunteers to share. Repeat.

Return to the Simile Overload demonstration page. Reveal the three sentences about things that can be heard. Highlight the simile following each "sense" sentence.

Once again, ask students to close their eyes and imagine themselves in a movie theater. Ask them to write a

sentence about something they hear. Then write a simile. Ask them to share with a partner and then ask for a few volunteers to share.

Step Three: Independent Practice

Choose one setting from the setting choices page. Students will describe the setting using their five senses. For this lesson, students will write as many similes as they can use the pattern that they just practiced. Offer a sticker (or other small reward) for each simile they use. This will cause students to overuse similes to the point of being ridiculous, but it is better to have more than less.

You can always pick and choose and edit if you have a lot of material. It is much harder to try to build a good piece of writing from only a few typical third-grade sentences.

Ask them to write ten to fifteen sentences.

When the writing is completed, collect the papers.

Step Four: Publishing

In this lesson, publishing doesn't mean completing a final copy. In this case, publishing means sharing with the class.

One at a time, read each paper out loud without identifying the author. Ask students to put one hand inside the other and hide them under their desks. On the hidden hand, students should count the number of similes they hear as you read each piece out loud.

When it is finished, ask students to hold up their fingers to show how many examples they counted. Let students compare this to the number that the teacher counted. Award the stickers to the student writer at this time.

Object Description Guide

Name _____What are you describing?

_____

Are you writing in a positive or negative way? _____

A. Write two words that tell how it looks.	D. Write two words that tell how it smells.
Write about something that it looks like. _____ _____	Write about something that smells like it. _____ _____
What does it make you think of? _____ _____	What does it make you think of? _____ _____
B. Write two words that tell how it smells. _____	E. Write two words that tell how it tastes. _____
Write about something that it smells like. _____ _____	Write about something that it tastes like. _____ _____
What does it make you think of? _____ _____	What does it make you think of? _____ _____
C. Write two words that tell how it feels. _____	F. Write two words that tell how it makes you feel inside. _____
Write about something that it feels like. _____	Tell something else that makes you feel that way. _____
What does it make you think of? _____ _____ _____	Can you think of another time when you felt that way? _____ _____

Similes Practice #1

Name _____

1. The baby was as noisy as _____

_____

2. The marble was tiny like _____

_____

3. The flowers smelled sweet like _____

_____

4. The sunset looked like _____

_____

5. The lion's breath smelled as bad as _____

_____

6. The little boy was as hungry as _____

_____

7. The pillow felt soft like _____

_____

8. The book was boring like _____

_____

9. The cake disappeared just like _____

_____

10. The girl's face turned white like _____

_____

Similes Practice #2

Name _____

1. The man's nose was as big as _____

_____

2. Her fingernails were as sharp as _____

_____

3. When he was sick, his face was as green as _____

_____

4. The tree shivered like _____

_____

5. The fire was hot like _____

_____

6. The smoke was as thick as _____

_____

7. The pickle was as sour as _____

_____

8. The new car was shiny like _____

_____

9. Her smile was as beautiful as _____

_____

10. The star was as bright as _____

_____

CONCEPT #3: WRITING A STORY

Foundation Information

A story is the most common form of fiction writing. A story consists of several components. The skills for writing each component should be taught individually before attempting to combine them.

Setting--This tells the reader the time and place in which the story occurs.

Problem and solution--These are the beginning and the end of the story.

Characters-- The characters are the people who live in a story. They solve the problem or sometimes try to keep it from being solved.

Plot--The plot consists of the events that occur between the problem and the solution.

The writing of stories involves four basic phases. In phase one, students will write a story before any instruction takes place so that each student's skills can be evaluated. In the second phase, the teacher will give basic instruction in the various components of a fiction story. In phase three, students will plan their story. In the fourth phase, students will follow the standard writing process and use their plan to write a story.

Lesson #10: Introduction to Story Writing (Find Out What They Know)

Before any instruction in writing fiction, it is important to find out what the students already know.

In this lesson, students will complete the pre-writing and rough draft stages of writing a story. They will be asked to do this with limited assistance from the teacher.

Students will write this story the first day of school. Students should write the date at the top of their papers.

At the beginning of third grade, a student should be able to write in complete sentences. Spelling may be phonetic, but should be decipherable. Does the story have a beginning, middle, and end? If not, those students may need extra help when independent practice begins. If a student uses dialog or vivid description, then they are more advanced than their peers.

Sort the papers into those who are going to need a lot of assistance, those who are okay, and those who are proficient.

Step One: Pre-write

Pre-writing is a critical phase of story writing. It should never be skipped. For this lesson, obtain a copy of *Grandfather's Pencil and the Room of Stories* by Michael Foreman (Harcourt Brace & Co., 1994). Copies are available for purchase from our website at www.KidsandWriting or from the public library. Read the story to the class.

Ask students to name all the new school supplies they brought or received at school. Record all answers. Then ask what might happen if one of their school supplies came alive? What problems would it cause?

Start with a single item like a pencil or a bottle of glue. Brainstorm for each item separately.

Here are some ideas to get you started:

- The pencil writes notes on your school papers.
- The pencil always writes the wrong answers.
- The glue refuses to come out of the bottle.
- Your lunch pail eats all of your lunch--and some other things.
- Your thermos belches every time you open it.
- Your eraser talks to you and gets you in trouble.
- Every time you blink, your paper folds itself into a paper airplane and takes off.
- Your binder snaps at your fingers when you try to get a piece of paper.

Once the students get started, they will think of lots and lots of ideas. Write them down. Set a time limit of 15-20 minutes for this activity.

Step Two: Write the Rough Draft

Distribute paper and ask students to choose one and only one of the problems on the board. Ask them to write a story about how they solve the problem. Tell them not to worry about spelling, but to do the best they can to sound out the words. Provide assistance if they ask.

Lesson #11: Plan the Story (2-3 days)

Even experienced authors plan their stories before they write them. Taking time to plan will make the writing process quicker and easier.

Step One: Choose the Problem

Students need to find a problem for their story. Below are two ways to help students find a problem for their story.

1. Students may choose a problem from one of the lists created and saved from the Problem and Solution lessons.

2. Use one of the planning pages from the book "Prewriting: More than Writing Prompts" by Julie Coan. This book is available at www.KidsandWriting.com.

Distribute a copy of the Plot Plan worksheet (p. 39) to each student. Students should write their story's problem in box #1 on the worksheet. Take a few minutes to meet with each student after they have finished.

Step Two: Choose the Main Character

Students need to choose a main character. They may choose one from the character profiles completed during the character lessons or complete an original character profile just for this story. (worksheet on p. 63)

Step Three: Plan the Plot

Ask students to follow the questions on the plot page. The answers don't need to be long--a sentence or two is fine.

Monitor students and assist those that need help. Some teachers like to meet with each student after they complete each block on the Plot Plan page.

Encourage students to come up with their own ideas. Remind them that the more difficult they make the plot, the more interesting the story is.

The two things that their character does to solve the problem (boxes two and four) should be very different from each other. For example, if a student writes "Joe hit the monster with a baseball bat" in the second square, then the fourth square should not read, "Joe hit the monster with a shovel".   In the fourth square, Joe should not hit him with anything: it's too similar. While it is not really wrong, it will make the story boring to write and boring to read. Perhaps Joe can set a trap for the monster or feed him something that makes him go to sleep.

When students write about the reason things don't work in boxes three and five, the story will be better if there is action. For example, after Joe hits the monster with the baseball bat, the student writes "He didn't do anything" in box three. That is not very interesting. Students won't want to write a whole scene about someone doing nothing and readers will not want to read it either. Encourage students to make the monster do something like eat all Joe's candy bars or steal his comic books.

Meet with each student and check the boxes in their plot plan. Then ask them to write the solution to the story in box #6.

Lesson #12: Scene Building
Practice Level 1

This lesson will focus on developing the skills needed to take the plot plan to a rough draft. These writing skills will be focused on the "action" part of the scene.

Step One: Direct Instruction
Teacher Script:

If you rode a roller coaster and it was over in two minutes, you'd ask for your money back. If you paid to go on the biggest roller coaster in the world and it turned out to be a little kiddie roller coaster, you'd be very upset. It wouldn't be fair.

That's what happens when you write a story and you don't add enough detail. Your readers will think it isn't fair. They were getting ready for a really good

story and instead they got the kiddie roller coaster.

Today we're going to practice adding detail to make your story really exciting.

Instruction

In this section, the questions that are asked by the teacher are in bold. There are many possible answers. One possible answer is provided.

On the board, write: Julio bought a candy bar.

Ask, **"What does Julio do first?"**

Keep asking, **"Is this the first thing?"** until you get to: Julio walked into the store.

Add a sentence describing the store. The store was big and bright. Julio knew it as well as his own house. He visited there every day with his mom.

Ask, **"What's he thinking about?"** Accept any answer that has something to do with buying a candy bar. It might be something like, "Julio's mouth watered as he thought about how good a candy bar would taste."

Then ask, **"What does he do next?"** He went to the candy aisle.

What did he see? He saw a Kit-Kat bar.

Ask, **"What is he thinking about?"** He liked the way it was crunchy and chocolate-y.

"What does he do next?" He picked up a bag of Gummi worms. They were round and squishy like spaghetti.

"What is he thinking about?" He liked the fruity flavor and the way they stretched out long. He didn't know which one to choose.

"What does he do next?" He decided to buy both. Then, he walked to the front of the store to the cashier.

"What is he thinking about?" He suddenly wondered if he had enough money.

"What does he do next?"
He sat down on the floor and pulled all the money out of his pocket and counted it.

Point out the pattern of the questions.

The pattern is:

1. What does he do next?
2. What does he hear, see, smell, touch, or taste?
3. What is he thinking about?

Like the Description Writing Guide, these questions don't need to be rigidly followed in order.

Step Two: Guided Practice

Distribute the Scene Writing Worksheet (p. 37). Walk them through Scene One by asking the pattern questions and waiting for students to write the reply. Ask for three or four volunteers to share their scenes.

Divide students into pairs. Each pair will work together to complete the Scene Two. Allow ten to fifteen minutes to complete the scene. Then, ask for three or four volunteers to share their scenes.

Step Three: Independent Practice

Students will complete the remainder of the worksheet independently.

Lesson #13 Write the Rough Draft (6-7 days)

The goal of the rough draft phase is to get the highest quality product in the shortest amount of time. In order to do this, instruction during the rough draft phase must be one-on-one. For successful, stress-free classroom management, use the management technique outlined on p.35.

All rough drafts should be written on the front of the piece of paper only, leaving the back blank for revision at a later time. Every page should be numbered to avoid confusion and the student's name should be written at the top of each page.

A teacher needs to strike a careful balance between creation and revision during this phase. Resist the urge to tell students to rewrite a scene during the rough draft phase. If something major is missing or the scene is not long enough, the teacher should suggest ways to add on to the scene. (Don't worry if things are slightly out of order in the story; this will get fixed during the revising phase.)

After students write each scene of the story, they will meet with the teacher. Discuss with them what will happen in the next scene. You can make a few brief notes in the margin to remind the student what was discussed. Always refer to the student's Plot Plan. Students should get used to using this as a guide. At some point, students will be able to follow this independently.

Step One: Write the Setting

Most stories and books begin with a description of the setting. That's because this helps the reader see the story in their mind's eye.

Therefore, students should begin their story by writing a description of the setting. Once each student has finished their plan, they will describe the setting where the story begins. Remind them that they should use all their senses. They may follow the Descriptive Writing Chart, if they would like. The setting should be about half of a page long.

Step Two: Writing Scene by Scene

After the setting, the student will write a scene for each box on the plot plan page. Each scene should be about half a page in length. This is a guideline only.

The teacher should meet and confer with each student after each scene is completed. When looking at the scene, look for things that need improvement. For instance, if the student is not giving enough detail or is not using sensory details, make suggestions for improvement that will be used in the next scene.

Some students may copy exactly what is on the plan page. They may come to a conference with a scene that is only two sentences long. Rely often on the roller coaster analogy. Remind them of the scene writing practice they recently completed.

3 Areas to Focus on During Conferences

There are three areas that students can improve on as they write from scene to scene. Choose one or two at a time for the student to improve.

1. Telling the scene in a few sentences
The scene moves too quickly. Remind students that you get the roller coaster effect by slowing down and writing about the small details of the action of the scene.

2. Lack of sensory detail
Students must use their five senses. What is the character seeing, smelling, hearing, touching, and tasting?

3. Lack of "feeling" sentences
If a scene seems like it contains enough detail and it still seems like something's missing, check to see if the student wrote about how the character was feeling and what he/she was thinking about.

Don't worry about grammar and spelling at this point. The main goal is to get a high-quality rough draft with lots of description.

Lesson #14: Revise the Story (2 days)

When students revise their stories, they will be focusing on improving the content of their stories. Young students will generally only be able to focus on one form of revision at a time. This means that students will actually need to work through their story several times, revising something different each time.

Revisions should be written on the back of the paper where they are to be inserted. They should be numbered and the same number should be inserted into the story at the location the revision needs to be added.

Try not to make this a painful process. If students are able to improve three or four parts of their story, that's a good beginning. At first, the teacher may have to help students locate places in the story that need revision.

During their first revision, students should search each scene for places where they can add sensory details about what they see, hear, smell, touch, and taste.

During their second revision, students should look for places where their character does something or where something happens to their character. They should make sure that they explain in detail what their character is feeling

Lesson #15: Edit the Story

Read about editing on p. 132.

Lesson #16: Final Copy (2-3 days)

Students will write a final copy of their story.

Lesson #17: Choosing the Title

Read about choosing the title on p. 133.

The Reading Connection

As students read books during the year, they should identify the characters, the setting(s), the problem and the solution, and the plot of the stories they read. Use stories that have a strong up and down motion in the plot, so that students can actually record each plot shift on a small piece of paper. Then the student can create a poster showing the up and down motion of the plot.

Books that work well for this are:
Space Scooter by Brent Filson
The Snack Attack Mystery by Elizabeth Levy

Classroom Management for Writing

Here are some suggestions to increase students' efficiency and make classroom management easier.

Problem: Students wait too long in line.

Solution:

When writing a story, you must hold individual writer's conferences and give individual help. To avoid a long line of students standing at the teacher's desk waiting for help, place a "Help" list up on the board on which students write their name when they need assistance. Then call them up one at a time to give help.

Problem: Students don't sign up to conference.

Solution:

There may be students who never put their name on the Help List. On a class list, keep track of each student conference. If students are not signing up, there are several solutions.

1.   If there are just one or two students, call them up the next day before beginning the Help List.

2.   If there is a large group of students, have a day of writing where there is no Help List. Call each student up for an individual conference.

3. If there is a student who does not seem to be able to work independently, seat them near the conference area and check their writing often between conferences.

Problem: Students don't know what to do while they are waiting.

Solution:

An important rule to follow during writing time is that the only activity that is allowed during writing time is writing. Students should not be reading or drawing (unless it has to do with their writing) or talking. This problem will occur most often when a student's name is on the Help List and they are waiting for help.

One solution to this problem is to assign a separate independent writing assignment for students to work on while they are waiting. Although this solution works, it also distracts students from the story they are writing and it makes it difficult to re-focus when they are called for their conference. A better solution is to have them write an expansion assignment for the story that they are currently writing. This list can be written on the board or each student can keep a copy in their writing folders. You can find a list of ten expansion assignments on page 38.

Problem: Students lose their work.
Solution:

Collect students' writing every day. Stories that are kept in desks get lost too easily. It is worth the extra time it takes to collect the papers and give them back the next day.   Stories should be stored in individual folders. Stapling is not advisable until the story is finished.

Problem: There are problems with the help list.
Solution

Many problems with the Help List can be eliminated by teaching students to follow these simple rules.

Help List Rules:

1. No one erases anyone's name from the help list, including their own. If students take their name off when they're done, other students will write their names there and no one will know who's next on the list.

2. Students must bring every piece of their story every time they ask for help. This is an enormous time saver. A brief look at the plan will refresh your memory each time you meet with a student.

3. Each day at the beginning of the writing period, each student must read their entire story from the beginning and try to figure out what comes next on their own before adding their name to the help list.

4. Students must bring the story up to be checked after they have completed each box on the plot plan page.   Check off each box so that both teacher and student will know where they are. Take this opportunity to talk to them about the next box on the plan so that they have a general idea about what they are going to write before they go back to their desk. Sometimes it helps to make notes in the margin.

Scene Writing Worksheet

Name _____

Directions: Write 5 sentences that tell more about each action.

Scene One: Jacob looked all over the house for his lost cat.

_____

_____

_____

_____

_____

Scene Two: Emma was being chased by her sister and hid behind the

tree. _____

_____

_____

_____

_____

Scene Three: Daniel tried to lift the heavy bat so he could hit the baseball.

_____

_____

_____

_____

_____

Scene Four: Sophia went to her first dance lesson and was very clumsy.

_____

_____

_____

_____

_____

Expansion Assignments for Writing

1. Write a character profile for each of the characters in your story.

2. Describe your main character's house.

3. Draw a picture of your main characters wearing their favorite clothes.

4. Write a setting description for each location in which your story takes place.

5. Write a conversation between two of your characters about how to solve the problem. (Or a character can talk to himself.)

6. Make a list of different solutions to the problem in the story. They can be completely outrageous.

7. Describe each character's most prized possession.

8. What are the best things that have ever happened to each character?

9. What are the worst things that have ever happened to each character?

10. Write 10 similes that could be used in your story.

Name

Plot Plan Page

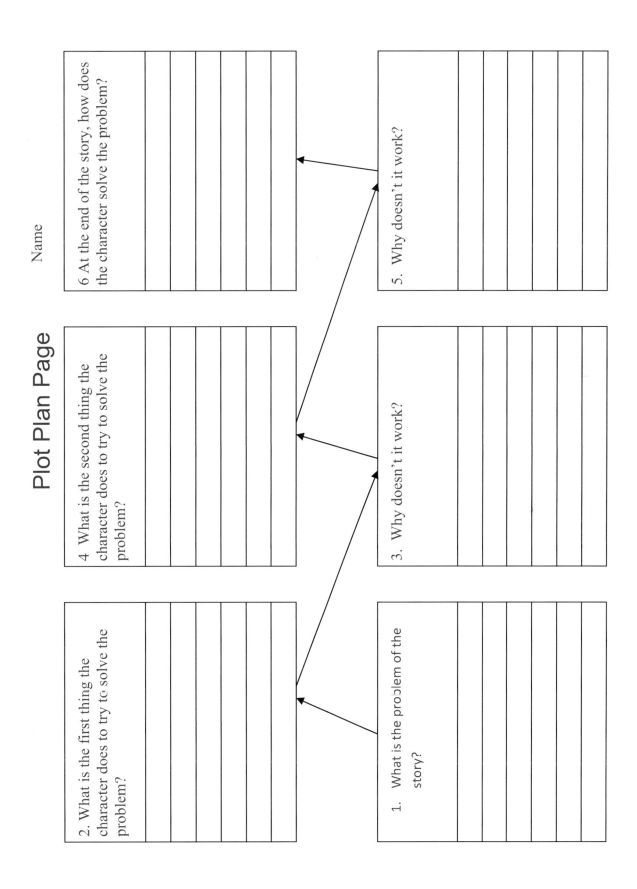

6 At the end of the story, how does the character solve the problem?

5. Why doesn't it work?

4 What is the second thing the character does to try to solve the problem?

3. Why doesn't it work?

2. What is the first thing the character does to try to solve the problem?

1. What is the problem of the story?

CONCEPT #3: WRITING A STORY
PART 1: THE SETTING

Foundation Information

Since most pieces of fiction begin with a description of the setting, it is a good place to begin teaching students to be authors. The setting of a story is the place or places where events in the story occur. However, if you picked up a book and it started, "This story happened in New York", you probably wouldn't read much farther.

The beginning of any story must suck the reader in like a giant vacuum cleaner. Students need to know that this is the main reason why kids (or anybody else) read fiction books to begin with. Readers want to be part of the story. For a short time, they get to become the character in the book. They get to solve a mystery or visit a chocolate factory, have a secret garden, become a wizard, or walk on Saturn's rings.

So how do authors do that? How do they make a reader feel like they're in a creepy basement, a magical castle, a baseball stadium, or the plains of Mars? It sounds a bit mysterious, or magical, but by focusing on the correct techniques and providing plenty of practice, even young students can "suck you in" with amazing skill.

To describe a setting effectively, a writer must fool the reader's senses so that the reader believes he is elsewhere. Describing the setting of a story must begin by using the five senses.

Lesson #18: Introducing the Setting

Step One: Review the Five Senses

Begin by reviewing the five senses. Most students are aware of these from lessons in the earlier grade levels.

Step Two: Get Ready to Write

Choose a location outside the classroom where you can take students to describe their setting.

Students will write the words, "hear, see, smell, feel, and taste" at the top of their paper. Supply each student with a clipboard (a workbook fitted with a binder clip or large paper clip can be used instead).

Set these rules before leaving the classroom:

1. There can be absolutely no talking.

2. You must sit at least five feet from any other student.

3. Don't spend too long thinking. Write the first thing that comes into your mind and don't stop writing until the teacher says stop.

4. You don't have to write in order. You can write about what you see first, then taste, and then come back and write another sentence about what you see.

5. Write in complete sentences, but write as much as you can.

Step Three: Describing the Setting

Take the students outside into the schoolyard, preferably when there are no other students outside. (If this isn't possible, choose another location on campus like the cafeteria or a hallway or a staircase.)

Let students get settled. Then say, "Ready, set, write!" Teachers are strongly advised to write with their students to set a good example. Students should write for fifteen to twenty minutes. Give students a warning signal about three minutes before time is up so that

they can finish the sentence they are working on or the thought they are in the middle of.

Step Four: Share

When you get back to the classroom, offer students an opportunity to share their writing. Some students' writing will sound something like a grocery list. That's okay. It will improve rapidly. Listen carefully and choose one or two good details to point out to the class when they are finished. For example: "I like the way Mary wrote about how the clouds looked like a storm was coming. " or "The reason we laughed when Bret wrote about how the ants tap-danced on his leg was because that was an example of excellent writing." The class should be encouraged to applaud every writer's effort regardless of their opinion of how good or bad they think it is.

Make sure students write their name and the date on their papers. Add these to your students' writing portfolios.

Lesson #19: Describing the Setting— Guided Practice

The students will help the teacher write a new setting. Choose a setting that the students will be familiar with, and yet still be excited about. A jungle setting or a setting in a McDonald's restaurant are excellent choices to start with.

Ask students to visualize themselves standing in the setting. Ask, "What do you see?" Give them a minute to think. Ask them to give replies in the form of a complete sentence. Draw them into giving more detailed sentences. For instance, if a student says, "I see a giant snake", ask what the snake is doing. Then write "I see a giant snake slithering through the trees."

After each sense sentence, ask all students, "How does that make you feel?" The snake makes me want to run and hide under my bed.

Example: "I hear the leaves crunch"

"Why are the leaves crunching?" "I hear the leaves crunch as something sneaks toward me."

"How does that make you feel?"

"I am so scared that I am shaking and my knees are knocking together."

Write the completed sentence on the board or on chart paper.

After writing several sentences for seeing, proceed to the other senses. Each time, the students should visualize the setting. Teachers should feel free to

add sentences or parts of sentences. A teacher may also ask students to lengthen their sentences. The goal is to create a good model for their writing.

After the setting is finished, show them that the basic pattern is:
A. Sense sentence
B. Feeling Sentence (How does it make you feel?)

Choose blue and green markers. With students' help underline the sense sentences in blue and the feeling sentences in green so that they can see the pattern.

Lesson #20: Describing the Setting-- Practice Level 1

Step One: Descriptive Writing Direct Instruction

A description of the setting of a story is a form of fiction writing. It is how fiction stories begin. It is written by using the five senses and writing about how those things make you feel.

Distribute a copy of the Descriptive Writing Chart #1 (p. 56). Review the chart with students. Ask students to take out blue and green crayons or colored pencils. As you review the page, ask students to underline the sense questions with blue and the feeling questions in green. Show them the pattern of the sentences.

Step Two: Guided Practice

Distribute copies of the description of the setting titled *In the Desert* (p.52). Read the question 1a from the Chart. Ask students to find a sentence in the description that tells what you might see. Students should underline the sentence in blue. Read question 1b from the Chart. Ask students to find a sentence that describes a feeling. Students should underline the sentence in blue.

Read the question 2a from the Chart. Ask students to find a sentence in the description that tells what you might hear. Students should underline the sentence in blue. Read question 2b from the Chart. Ask students to find a sentence that describes a feeling. Students should underline the sentence in blue.

Step Three: Independent Practice

Students should continue to repeat this process for questions three through five. NOTE: Students should save Descriptive Writing Chart #1 for use with Lesson #21.

Lesson #21: Describing the Setting-- Practice Level 2

Step One: Descriptive Writing Direct Instruction

A description of the setting of a story is a form of fiction writing. It is how fiction stories begin. It is written by using the five senses and writing about how those things make you feel.

Review the Descriptive Writing Chart #1 used in Lesson #20. Review the pattern. Remind students that the sense questions are underlined in blue and the feeling questions are underlined in green.

Emphasize that this is only a guide. Although in this lesson, they will follow the questions in number order, they do not need to be written in the order they appear on the chart. They might write two number one sentences, then a number four sentence, and then two number three sentences.

This is not meant to be a worksheet, but a safety net. The goal is for students to internalize the pattern and be able to write without using the chart.

Step Two: Guided Practice

Students will write the description of a setting. Distribute a piece of lined paper to each student and ask students to place it next to the Descriptive Writing Chart #1. Choose a single setting from the Setting Choices Page for the entire class to write about. The sample setting should be placed where students can refer to as they write. "At the beach", "In the mountains", or "By the river" works well for this assignment. Choose a place that most of the students will be familiar with.

Ask students to imagine that they are standing in the setting that you chose. Read the first question from the Chart. Ask students to write a sentence about what they might see. After a minute or two, read the second question from the Chart. Tell students to write a sentence about how they feel about that sense. Ask volunteers to read their first two sentences. Repeat this process for questions 2a and 2b.

Step Three: Independent Practice

Students should write a sentence answering questions 3a through 5b.
NOTE: Students should save Descriptive Writing Chart #1 for use with Lesson #22.

Lesson #22: Describing the Setting-- Practice Level 3

In this lesson, students will only write through the rough draft stage. The lesson will continue to focus on the descriptive writing pattern introduced in Lesson #19.

Step One: Descriptive Writing Direct Instruction

A description of the setting of a story is a form of fiction writing. It is how fiction stories begin. It is written by using the five senses and writing about how those things make you feel.

Review the Descriptive Writing Chart #1 used in Lesson #20. Review the pattern. Remind students that the sense questions are underlined in blue and the feeling questions are underlined in green.

Step Two: Guided Practice

Students will write the description of a setting. Distribute a piece of lined paper to each student and ask students to place it next to the Descriptive Writing Chart #1. Choose a single setting from the Setting Choices Page (p. 55) for the entire class to write about. This setting should be different from the one used in the previous lesson. Choose a place that most of the students will be familiar with.

Remind students that the Chart is only a guide. The questions can be answered in any order. Students might write two number one sentences, then a number four sentence, and then two number three sentences. When they answer the questions, they must write two sentences, answering both the *a* and *b* questions. For example, if a student is answering #2, they would write a sentence for 2a and a sentence for 2b.

Ask a random student to choose a number between one and five. Then, ask students to imagine that they are standing in the setting that you chose. Read the question the student chose from the Chart. Ask students to write a sentence for the *a* and *b* questions. After a couple of minutes, ask volunteers to read both of their sentences. Repeat this process once more, using a different sense question.

Step Three: Independent Practice

Students should write at least ten more sentences independently. They should mix up the numbers and they should not use the same number twice in a row.

Lesson #23: Describing the Setting— Practice Level 4

In this lesson, students will use similes as part of their description. They will complete the entire writing process, including revising to focus and completion of a final draft.

Step One: Direct Instruction

Review these facts with students. The setting is a form of fiction writing. It is how fiction stories begin. It is written by using the five senses and writing about how those things make you feel.

Distribute a copy of the Descriptive Writing Chart #2 (p. 57) to each student. This will replace the Descriptive Writing Chart #1 that students have been using. Teachers may want to make a poster-sized copy to permanently display in the classroom.

Review the chart with students. Ask students to take out blue, green, and red crayons or colored pencils. With students' help, locate the sense questions and underline them in blue. Then locate the feelings questions and underline them in green. Finally, locate all of the simile questions and underline them in red.

Step Two: Guided Practice

Students will describe a setting

independently. If you feel comfortable with handling multiple topics, copy three or four topics from the Settings Choice list (p. 55) onto the board and allow students to choose one. Otherwise, assign a single setting from the list.

Distribute a piece of lined paper for each student. Students should place the Descriptive Writing Chart #2 on their desk next to their paper.

Emphasize that this is only a guide. This is not a worksheet, but a safety net. Just like Chart #1, the questions do not need to be written in the order they appear on the chart. However, the questions should be answered in sets of three. If the student chooses seeing, they should answer questions 1a, 1b, and 1c before choosing the next sense.

Randomly choose a sense to start with. (You can choose it by rolling dice if you wish.) Then, ask students to imagine that they are standing in the setting that you chose. Ask students to write three sentences that answer questions a, b, and c. Choose several students to share their sentences.

Step Three: Independent Practice

Students should write about fifteen more sentences (about half a page of lined paper), but emphasize that quality is more important that quantity.

If a student forgets how to describe a setting, they can refer back to the Descriptive Writing Chart #2. At first, they may follow this page precisely, because it makes it easier for them, but they need to learn to move past that. They should write down the ideas as they come to them but continue to use the five senses and similes and feelings statements when they write. This happens at a different rate for each child. By the end of the year, most students will no longer need the chart.

Step Four: Revise to Focus

When the setting description is used as an independent piece of writing, the goal is slightly different than a setting that is part of a story. If the setting is part of a story, it is revised with the theme of the story in mind. When it is meant to be an independent composition, it needs to contain its own focus. Because this technique is used for all independent forms of composition, it is described on p. 128.

Step Five: Revise Sentence Structure

In this step, students will revise the

sentence structure in their setting description.

When students first learn to describe the setting, nearly all their sentences with begin with the word "I". A full page of writing should contain only five or six sentences that begin with "I". All the rest should be changed.

Prior to completing this step for the first time, please complete lesson #24.

Step Six: Edit

Edit with students for spelling and grammar mistakes. Read about editing on p. 132.

Step Seven: Final Draft

Students will write a final draft.

Step Eight: Students should choose a title. Read about choosing a title on p. 133.

Step Nine: Illustrate

Students may illustrate, if you wish.

Step Ten: Publish

Read about five ways to publish students' writing on p. 134.

Lesson #24: Revising the Sentence Structure

Step One: Direct Instruction

Show students the top part of the Sentence Structure Demonstration Page (p. 53). Read it out loud. Ask students if they notice anything about the sentences. Most students should notice that most of the sentences begin with the word, "I". They may also notice that most of the sentences have a similar rhythm. They're kind of short and choppy.

The reason we revise the sentence structure is to improve the sound of the writing. To do that, students will change some of the sentences so that they no longer begin with "I" and combine some of the sentences to create longer sentences.

Reveal the second part of the Sentence Structure Revision Page. Read the paragraph aloud.

Point out how the "I" sentences were changed by beginning the sentence with the object of the sentence.

Reveal the examples at the bottom of the page. Show students how the process works.

- I saw moss growing in the trees. It looked like a mermaid's hair.
- I smelled the water in the pond. It smelled like dirty socks.

- I heard the bridge squeaking. It sounded like an old door opening.
- I touched the ocean water. It was as warm as a bath.
- I saw the woman standing there. She looked like an overgrown bat.
- I tasted the frosting on the cupcake. It tasted like mud.
- I heard the door slam shut. It was as loud as a car crash.

Step Two: Guided Practice

One at a time, ask students to revise the following sentences by eliminating the word "I" at the beginning of the sentence and combining the two sentences into one. Students can write their answers on paper or white boards. Check students' answers after each example.

Step Three: Independent Practice

Distribute Revising Sentence worksheet (p. 54). Students will complete the worksheet independently.

Lesson #25: The Third Person Setting
Practice Level 5

Step One: Direct Instruction

When the setting is written as part of a story, it's generally written in the third person. In this lesson, students will learn to write their setting description in the third person. Reveal the first sentence of the Third Person Demonstration Page (p. 58).

Teach students that sentences written in the first person usually begin with the word "I" and are written from the narrator's point of view. Reveal the second sentence. Show students that sentences written in the third person often begin with someone's name or the pronouns he, she, or it. (PowerPoint presentation available online.)

Step Two: Guided Practice

One at a time, reveal the Guided Practice Sentences. After each one, ask students to rewrite the sentence on a white board or paper so that the sentence is written in the third person. Check student responses.

Step Three: Independent Practice

Distribute lined paper to each student. Choose three or four settings from the settings choice list and write them on the board. Allow students to choose one as their topic.

Students will describe this setting as if they were another person. Their first sentence should be something like, "_____was standing in the forest." Remind them to write using the five senses.   There should be a copy of Descriptive Writing Chart #2 available for students' use.   An individual copy for each student or a poster-sized copy for the class is acceptable.

Step Four: Revise Sentence Structure

Students should revise the sentence structure during this step.   Make sure all of the sentences are written in the third-person point of view.   Most of them will probably start with the character's name or he or she.   That's perfectly acceptable at this point.

Step Five: Edit

Edit with students for spelling and grammar mistakes. (p. 132)

Step Six: Final Draft

Students will write a final draft.

Step Seven: Choose a title (p. 133).

Step Eight: Illustrate

Students may illustrate, if you wish.

Step Nine: Publish

Read about five ways to publish students' writing on p. 134.

Lesson #26: Describing the Setting-- Practice Level 6

Step One: Gather Materials

Gather a collection of landscape pictures.   Pictures from calendars work well.   If they are laminated, they can be used every year.   There should be a picture for each student.

Step Two: Rough Draft

Distribute one of the pictures and a piece of lined paper to each student. Students will describe the setting as if they are standing in the place shown in the picture.   Remind them to write using the five senses.   There should be a copy of the Descriptive Writing Chart #2 available for students' use.   Students may use either an individual copy or a poster- sized copy that is displayed in the class.

Step Three: Revise to Focus

When the setting description is used as an independent piece of writing, the goal is slightly different.   If the setting is part of a story, it is revised with the theme of the story in mind.   When it is meant to be an independent composition, it needs to contain its own focus.

Because this technique is used for all independent forms of composition, it is described on p. 130.

Step Four: Revise Sentence Structure

When students first learn to describe the setting, nearly all their sentences with begin with the word "I". Over time, students will learn to vary their sentence structure as they write. Until then, ask students to revise the sentence structure during this step. A full page of writing should contain only five or six sentences that begin with "I". All the rest should be changed. If students are having difficulty, suggest that they begin their sentence with the object of the sentence.

Step Five: Edit

Edit with students for spelling and grammar mistakes. (p. 132)

Step Six: Final Draft

Students will write a final draft.

Step Seven: Choose a Title

Students should choose a title for their work. Read about choosing a title on page 133.

Step Eight: Illustrate

Students may illustrate their writing.

Step Nine: Publish

Read about five ways to publish students' writing (p. 134).

Lesson #27: Cross-curricular Settings

Step One: Review

Choose a setting from the class's science or social studies curriculum. For instance, if the class is studying space, the teacher might ask students to describe what it would be like to stand on the moon or in a space ship. If the class was studying flowers, students could describe what it is like to be a bee landing on a flower.

Ask students to locate their Descriptive Writing Chart #2 or place it in a location where it is easily visible to the entire class.

Choose a sample of student writing that demonstrates how a good description should be written. The sample can be placed on a smart board or overhead where it can be viewed by all students. Make individual copies for each student.

Ask each student to take out red, blue, and green crayons or colored pencils. In the student sample, ask students to locate a sense sentence and underline it in blue. Randomly choose two students to share a sense sentence they found.

In the student sample, ask students to locate a sentence that describes a feeling and underline it in green. Randomly choose two students to share a feeling sentence they found.

In the student sample, ask students to locate a simile and underline it in red. Randomly choose two students to share a simile they found.

Ask students to underline the remaining sense sentences with blue, the feeling sentences in green, and the similes in red.

Step Two: Rough Draft

Students may describe this setting in either first or third person. Remind them to write using the five senses. There should be a copy of the Descriptive Writing Chart available for students' use. Either an individual copy for each student or a poster-sized copy for the class will work.

Step Three: Revise to Focus

Students should revise and focus their work. See Revise to Focus (p. 128)

Step Four: Revise Sentence Structure

Students should revise the sentence structure during this step. A full page of writing should contain only five or six sentences that begin with "I". All the rest should be changed.

Step Five: Edit

Edit with students for spelling and grammar mistakes. (p. 132)

Step Six: Final Draft

Students will write a final draft.

Step Seven: Students will choose a title.

Read about choosing a title on p. 133.

Step Eight: Illustrate

Students may illustrate, if you wish.

Step Nine: Publish

Read about five ways to publish students' writing on page 134.

In the Desert

The ground is brown and cracked. It makes me think of mud pies. I hear the wind whooshing in my ears. It sounds like a big fan blowing. I feel the sand blowing on my legs. It feels rough like sandpaper. I smell sweat. It smells like my dad after he mows the lawn. I taste hot air. It reminds me of the air in a popcorn maker.

Simile Overload

In a Movie Theater

I was sitting in a movie theater. I saw rows of heads in front of me. They looked like prairie dogs sticking their heads out of their holes. I saw a big white screen. It looked like a blank book. I saw popcorn. It looked like snowflakes. I heard the movie screen buzz as it changed sizes. It sounded like a swarm of angry bees. I heard shoes scratching on the cement floor. They sounded like tree branches scratching on my window. I heard people slurping their drinks. It sounded like the bathtub draining.

Sentence Structure Demonstration Page

In the Closet

I look in the closet. I see a pair of old tennis shoes with holes in the bottom. They look like little lost children. I feel sad because I liked those shoes. I remember when I ran a marathon in those shoes. I see lots of empty plastic hangers hanging on the bar. They look like tree branches that have lost all their leaves. I wonder where all the colorful clothes have gone. I smell dust. It smells like dirty socks. I wrinkle my nose.

In the Closet

I look in the closet. There is an old pair of tennis shoes lying in the corner. They look like little lost children. They make me feel sad because I liked those shoes.   I remember when I ran a marathon in those shoes. The empty plastic hangers look like tree branches that have lost their leaves. I wonder where all the colorful clothes have gone. The dust smells like dirty socks and it makes me wrinkle my nose.

Examples

Rough: I smell <u>the flowers</u>. They smell like perfume.

Revised: <u>The flowers</u> smell like perfume.

Rough: I hear the <u>lion's roar</u>. It sounds like a jet taking off.

Revised: The <u>lion's roar</u>   sounds like a jet taking off.

Revising the Sentence Structure

Rewrite these sentences so that they are a single sentence that doesn't start with the word "I".

1. I heard a song playing on the radio. It sounded like monkeys howling.

   _____

2. I smelled the cookie. It smelled like an old drain.

   _____

3. I saw the cat's eyes. They shone like emeralds in the sunlight.

   _____

4. I heard the cola sizzle. It reminded me of fireworks.

   _____

5. I tasted the wind. It was fresh and clean like clean towels.

   _____

6. I saw the bricks. They were stacked like a baby's building blocks.

   _____

7. I saw the toys on the floor. They were scattered like rocks by the river.

   _____

8. I touched the tree's bark. It felt rough like an alligator's skin.

   _____

9. I smelled the newly sharpened pencils. They reminded me of the first day of school.

   _____

10. I touched the wet sponge. It felt like raw hamburger.

   _____

11. I heard the wet shoes plop on the floor. They sounded like the banging of drums.

   _____

12. I heard the children yelling. They were as loud as a rock music band.

   _____

SETTING CHOICES

On a train

In a grocery store

In a McDonald's

In Australia

At the zoo

In a bakery

On a spider web

In a garden

On the freeway

In an ice cream parlor

On a lake

On a farm

On a bridge

In a jungle

In an Indian village

In the forest

At the fair

At a 7-11

In the forest

In (your town)

In San Francisco (or other
large city close by)

In a castle

On the beach

Under the ocean

In a space ship

In a mouse hole

In a cafeteria

By a pond

At a birthday party

In a doll house

In a haunted house

In a swimming pool

In a storm

In a volcano

In your backyard at night

In the fog

In a snowstorm

Descriptive Writing Chart #1

1a.**What do you <u>see</u>?**

1b.How does it make you feel? *or* What do you think about when you see it?

2a. **What do you <u>hear</u>?**

2b. How does the sound make you feel? *or* What do you think about when you hear it?

3a. **What can you <u>touch</u>?**

3b. How does it make you feel? *or* What do you think about when you touch it?

4a. **What do you <u>smell</u>?**

4b. How does it make you feel? *or* What do you think about when you smell it?

5a. **What can you <u>taste</u>?**

5b. How does it make you feel? *or* What do you think about when you taste it?

Repeat any of these as many times as you wish.

Descriptive Writing Chart #2

1a.**What do you <u>see</u>?**

1b. What does it look like? (use a simile)

1c. How does it make you feel? *or* What do you think about when you see it?

2a. **What do you <u>hear</u>?**

2b. What does it sound like? (use a simile)

2c. How does the sound make you feel? *or* What do you think about when you hear it?

3a. **What can you<u> touch</u>?**

3b. What does it feel like? (use a simile)

3c. How does it make you feel? *or* What do you think about when you touch it?

4a. **What do you <u>smell</u>?**

4b. What does it smell like? (use a simile)

4c. How does it make you feel? *or* What do you think about when you smell it?

5a. **Do you <u>taste</u> anything?**

5b. What does it taste like? (use a simile)

5c. How does it make you feel? *or* What do you think about when you taste it?

Repeat any of these as many times as you wish.

Third Person Setting Demonstration Page

First Person—

I was sitting on the beach. I looked up at the sky. It was as blue as a robin's egg.

Third Person—

Jack was sitting on the beach. He looked up at the sky. It was as blue as a robin's egg.

Guided Practice Sentences

1. I ran in the sand along the beach.

2. I thought the grass felt like green toothpicks.

3. It made me shiver.

4. I could smell the dust that made me sneeze.

5. The waves licked at my toes and made me laugh.

CONCEPT #3: WRITING A STORY
PART 2: CHARACTER DEVELOPMENT

Foundation Information

At the third grade level, character development is not a priority. However, a story cannot exist without characters. It is therefore important that there are some lessons about characters. The creation of a person on paper seems like magic. When a writer starts, there is nothing. When the writer finishes, a person exists on paper who speaks and thinks. This person has feelings, worries, likes, and dislikes. The reader can tell how this person will act in a particular situation. In other words, from thin air and imagination, the writer has created a person who seems alive.

Character Development: Key Teaching Points

1. Characters in stories are not like people in real life. They are much simpler.

2. Characters in stories are identified by one or two main characteristics. Give them an unusual habit and an unusual look.

3. Don't forget basic information. What is their name? How old are they?

What kind of family do they live with? What kind of house do they live in? What do they like to do best? What do they hate? Do they have any bad habits?

4. Don't let students use their names or the names of people they know (either real or fictional) as their characters' names. There are two very good reasons for this and students should be aware of these reasons so they understand why the rule exists.

First, there is a possibility of embarrassing someone or hurting their feelings. Most students would not do this intentionally, but sometimes, in order to further the story, the character must do something that is not very nice. If the student author has to worry about whether or not they are going to hurt someone's feelings or embarrass someone, they may actually change the events of the story and it may not turn out to be as good a story as it could have been.

The second reason is that if a student chooses the name of someone they know, they already have an idea in their head about what that person is like.

They know what they look like and how they talk and act. Because they know all that, it will make it more difficult to choose which traits to include in their story. The character will turn out unclear and uninteresting in the story.

Lesson #28: Character Profile Introduction

Step One: Preparation

In preparation for this activity, you will need to search magazines for photographs of people. The more unusual the pictures, the easier it will be for the students to write something interesting about them. Don't use pictures of famous or well-known people. Cut the pictures out. If they are mounted on tag board and laminated, they can be used year after year.

Step Two: Introduction

Distribute one of the pictures and a copy of the Character Profile #1 worksheet (p. 63) to each student. Divide students into groups of four. For this exercise, students will need to pretend that they are the person in the picture. Remind students that they want their characters to be interesting so they should take some time to think of interesting

answers. They shouldn't write down the first thing that pops in to their heads.

Use the script below. Ask the first three questions one at a time, giving students time to create their answers between each one. At the teacher's signal, students will pass both the paper and the picture to the person on their right. The teacher will read numbers five and six on the script. Then, students will again pass both paper and the picture to the person on their right. Repeat the process until all the questions have been answered.

Script to use with Character Profile worksheet:

1. What is your name? (Students shouldn't use their real name and should follow the classroom rules for character names.)

2. How old are you? Look at the picture and make a guess. (There are no wrong answers. A student may write 102 for the age of a child, which might seem incorrect. However, if the character was a child who had been placed under a spell or possibly was an alien, that answer could be correct.)

3. Where do you live? You can choose any city or country, but it might also be a kind of place instead, like a cave or a

mansion, or even the washing machine.

4. Who do you live with? Tell about the other people (and/or animals) that live in your house.

PASS YOUR PAPER AND PHOTOGRAPH TO THE PERSON ON YOUR RIGHT.

5. What do you look like? Describe hair color and clothes and anything else you can think of including the wart on your nose and the tattoo on your arm. You can tell about the big bruise your brother gave you when he punched you in the arm and the hair growing in your ears. Make sure your description fits the person you see in the photograph.

6. Name a bad habit that you have? Look for clues in the photograph PASS YOUR PAPER AND PHOTOGRAPH TO THE PERSON ON YOUR RIGHT.

7. What do you love to do? Look for clues in the photograph.

8. What do you hate? Look for clues in the photograph.

PASS YOUR PAPER AND PHOTOGRAPH TO THE PERSON ON YOUR RIGHT.

9. What did you do last Saturday? Look for clues in the photograph. How do you feel about it? Why did you do it?

10. What have you always wanted to do?

Look for clues in the photograph. How long have you wanted to do it? Why do you want to do it?

Step Three: Share

When all students have finished, students will stand up one at a time and share their photograph and introduce their character.

Lesson #29: Character Profile: Guided Practice

Step One: Brainstorm

With the class, brainstorm a list of words that tell how people can act. Record the list on chart paper so it can be used over and over again. A sample list of character traits is provided on p. 64 for your reference.

Step Two: Choose Three Traits

Use chart paper, the chalkboard, a smart board, or an overhead projector. Choose a name, adhering to the classroom naming rules. Write the character's name at the top. Then choose three students to choose a character trait from your class's list. The traits must be compatible with each other. If one student chooses happy, the next student can't choose sad. Write the three chosen traits next to the name.

Step Three: Create the Character

    With students' help, the teacher will create a character. Begin with one of the chosen traits. Ask students what the character might do that would show that he/she has that trait. For example, if one of the traits chosen was silly, then students would suggest something that the character does that shows that they are silly. Students might suggest: Millie wears red polka dot pants and large yellow shoes. Millie turns cartwheels when she is happy.

    Feel free to modify or lengthen the students' sentences. This gives the teacher a chance to model good writing. Repeat the process with the other two traits. When you are finished, read the finished product to the students. Display this model until after lesson #30.

Lesson #30: Character Profile: Independent Practice

Step One: Three Character Traits

    Students will create a character on their own. They may not use any of the characters, traits, or ideas already used in class. Ask them to start by choosing a character's name and writing it on the top of their paper. Then they should choose three traits from the class list. Students should decide whether their character is a good guy or a bad guy. If the character is a good guy, then they should choose good traits. If the character is a bad guy, they should choose less desirable traits. Students should write a minimum of two sentences for each trait (about half of a page total).

Step Two: Character Profile

    Distribute a new Character Profile worksheet (p. 63) to each student. Students should complete the profile for the character that they described in step one.

Step Three: Draw the Character

    Students may draw a picture of their character.

Step Four: Publish

    Collect the Character Profile, the Character Trait Description, and the picture from each student. Assemble them into a single reference book so students can look at it any time they need help finding a good character for a story.

Character Profile #1

My character's name is _____

My character is _____ years old and lives in_____

_____

My character lives with _____

_____

What does your character look like? _____

_____

What are his or her favorite clothes?_____

Where is your character's favorite place to hang out? _____

What can your character do very well?_____

_____

What can't your character do very well?_____

_____

My character loves to _____

_____

My character hates _____

_____

What is your character afraid of?_____

_____

My character always wished they could _____

CHARACTER TRAITS

angry	funny	popular
athletic	fussy	powerful
attractive	graceful	prejudicial
beautiful	guilty	proud
bitter	gullible	resourceful
brave	happy	rich
caring	healthy	romantic
cautious	helpful	rotten
cheater	honest	rude
clumsy	impulsive	sad
complacent	indifferent	scheming
confused	innovative	selfish
cool	insane	serious
creative	irritated	shabby
curious	kind	shallow
dirty	liar	shrewd
disappointed	lonely	shy
dishonest	lucky	sick
dishonest	mean	skinny
dreamer	meddling	smart
dull	messy	sneaky
dumb	mischievous	starving
elegant	mysterious	stealthy
embarrassed	neutral	stern
energetic	nuisance	stingy
enthusiastic	old	strong
excited	old-fashioned	stubborn
far	perfect	suspicious
foolish	persistent	sweet
forgetful	pesty	systematic
friendly	plain	thoughtful
friendly	poor	trusting

CONCEPT #3 : WRITING A STORY
PART 3: PROBLEM AND SOLUTION

Foundation Information

The problem and solution of a fictional work are, simply stated, the beginning and the end of the story. The problem is presented within the first page of a short story. The character labors throughout the story to solve the problem, hopefully against terrible odds, and at the end of the story, finally overcomes those odds and solves the problem.

Lesson #31: Introduction to Problem and Solution

Step One: *The School Bus Story*

Begin by telling students the "School Bus Story" or feel free to make up your own equally inane version.

The School Bus Story

There was once a happy little school bus. He loved to carry all the happy children to school every day. He knew where each child lived. He would even start to slow down before the driver stepped on the brake. One day the regular bus driver retired and a new bus driver took his job. The new bus driver was nice and seemed to know all the stops. The happy little school bus knew he would be happy forever.

Use the following questions to lead a short discussion about the story:

How many of you liked the story?

How many of you thought the story was interesting and would like to hear what happens the next day?

What is the story missing?

Can anyone come up with a problem that might make this story more interesting? (Record several possible problems on the board.)

Can anyone come up with a possible solution for these problems? (Record these answers also.)

Step Two: Guided Practice

Read a short version of *Cinderella* to the students. Together, determine the problem of the story (Cinderella is a slave to her step-mother and step-sisters). Then, discuss the solution (Cinderella is taken to live in the castle).

Lesson #32: Problem and Solution-- Independent Practice

Step One: Read

Read "The Velveteen Rabbit" by Margery Williams to the class.

Step Two: Brainstorm

Write "stuffed rabbit" on a piece of chart paper. Write "real rabbit" underneath it. Ask the students to think of other things that a rabbit could be made of. Make a list. When they have exhausted this idea, also ask them what other kind of rabbits there might be. Record every answer. Later, choices can be limited by circling some and telling them that they must choose one that is circled. In this way, all answers are validated.

Some possibilities are:

a carved wooden rabbit

a rabbit in a painting

a glass rabbit

a rabbit bank

a ghost rabbit

a cloud rabbit

a rabbit constellation

a rabbit statue

a snow rabbit

a puppet rabbit

a robot rabbit

Step Three: Create the Problems

Choose one type of rabbit from the list. Ask the students to suggest problems that this rabbit might have.

For example: A stuffed rabbit may have lost his stuffing or been lost or abandoned.

A ghost rabbit may have forgotten how to go through walls.

A carved wooden rabbit might have termites or get broken.

Step Four: Create the Problem--Team Practice

From the list, choose two kinds of rabbits for each group of four students. Write each of the names on a separate piece of paper and place the names in a basket. Ask one student from each group to choose one. Pass out a small piece of chart paper to each group and ask them to talk together and see if they can come up with a problem that their rabbit might have.

After five minutes or so, ask the groups to share their results with the class. Then ask them to find a solution to the rabbit's problem. Tell them that the more unique the solution is, the more interesting their story will be. Give each group an opportunity to share their solutions.

Step Five: Create the Problem—Individual Practice

Ask one person from each group to choose a different type of rabbit from the basket.   This time students will work independently.   They should try to come up with as many problems as they can. After ten minutes, ask them to write a solution for each of their problems.

Step Six: Share

Ask students to take two minutes to circle their favorite problem and solution. Ask for volunteers to share their favorite problems and solutions.

Step Seven: Future Lessons

Keep all the lists of problems and solutions for future lessons.

CONCEPT #3: WRITING A STORY
PART 4: THE PLOT

Foundation Information

Plot, in its simplest and most basic form, takes the shape of a wave. This wave of action (also called the emotional wave) is the reason that we love to read books. It's a lot like riding a roller coaster. Children's books start with a very simple wave. As books get more and more complex, several waves overlap, bringing us strong emotional conflict.

It is important that students understand the basic idea of this format. They should use it as a format when they write and they need to identify it in the books that they read.

Lesson #33: Introduction to the Plot

Step One: Direct Instruction--The Up and Down Wave

Draw a large wave on the board with four crests and troughs. Trace the line and take a deep audible breath in as you move your pen to the top of the crest. Exhale audibly as you trace the line to the bottom of the trough. Repeat and ask the students to breathe in and out with you. Explain that this is how the basic plot of a story is written.

Step Two: Guided Practice--Up and Down in a Story

Next, tell the story of *Cameron and the Lake.* As you tell the story, use your hand to make the appropriate up and down wave motions as indicated in the story. When you are finished, repeat the story while pointing to the wave on the board and asking students to inhale and exhale in the appropriate places.

Cameron and the Lake

Cameron had tried for three summers to swim across the lake, but he had always had to turn back. This summer, he was determined to swim all the way across. He stretched his muscles and waded into the water. Only a few minutes had passed. He stopped and looked back. He was almost one third of the way there! (up)

He began to swim again, but a few

minutes later, the muscle in his leg began to cramp. It hurt so bad he could barely breathe. He started to panic and he started to sink. (down) Then he remembered that his brother had taught him to point his toe. He did it and the cramp went away. He floated on his back for a few minutes and then he began to swim again. Soon he was much closer to the other side. (up)

Then he felt something big and slippery grab onto his leg and pull him down. It felt like a shark! He was so close and now he was going to get eaten! (down)

Cameron kicked up hard and the thing let go. He swam to the surface and took deep gulps of air. A moment later his brother Bobby popped up beside him. "Ha, ha! Got ya!" he laughed. Cameron splashed his brother and yelled, "Not fair!" Then he started laughing, too. (up)

Cameron looked at the shore. He knew that nothing could stop him now. He swam the last fifty feet to the shore in only five minutes.

Step Three: Independent Practice

Distribute a copy of the story *The Perfect Cookie (p. 70)* to each student. Ask each student to write up or down on each line next to the appropriate parts of the story.

THE PERFECT COOKIE

Danielle was in the third grade and her favorite thing to do at home after school (other than homework) was to bake cookies.

One day, her mother showed her an announcement in the newspaper. It said, "Perfect Cookie Contest on November 3rd. First prize is $25.00."Danielle decided to enter the contest. She had three days to bake the perfect cookie.

Danielle thought that a rainbow cookie would be the perfect cookie. She mixed up the cookie dough. She added red, orange, yellow, blue, and green colors. She put the cookies in the oven. She was sure she would win the contest. Everyone loved rainbows._____

When Danielle pulled the cookies out of the oven, she got an ugly surprise. All the colors had mixed together and the cookies looked black. Danielle was very upset. She threw the cookies in the trash. _____

The next day, Danielle was eating cotton candy. She loved the way it melted in her mouth. Just then, she had an idea! She would put cotton candy in her perfect cookie so that it would melt in your mouth. She stirred some into her next batch of cookies. The cookies looked pink and delicious. She put them in the oven to bake. She could imagine the mayor giving her the first prize for the perfect cookie._____

When she pulled the cookies out of the oven, she was not happy at all. The cookies had melted together. The pan was filled with slimy pink ooze. "No!" she cried. "This can't be happening."_____

She was running out of time. She decided to bake her favorite peanut butter cookies. She was just getting ready to put them on the cookie trays when her mom reached in the cupboard and spilled a bottle of chocolate syrup into the bowl. There was no time to mix any more cookies. Danielle baked the cookies and won the prize._____

CONCEPT #4: WRITING PARAGRAPHS
PART 1: WEB TO PARAGRAPH

Foundation Information

Paragraphs are the basic building blocks of non-fiction writing. Students must be proficient at writing paragraphs before they can write any other form of non-fiction. Third grade students should write two or three paragraphs every week throughout the school year.

Lesson #34: Introduction to Paragraph Writing

Step One: Find Out What They Know

Write the following words on the board exactly as they are written here:

Lemonade is great to drink on a hot day. It will help cool you down. It is made from lemons, water, and sugar. Its sweet and sour taste is refreshing. It can be yellow or pink.

Read the sentences out loud. Ask students to raise their hands if they think that this is a paragraph. Ask students to raise their hands if they think that is isn't a paragraph. Ask students to raise their hand if they don't know.

Explain that this is not a paragraph. Ask students if they can tell the class why it is not a paragraph. Some students will probably say that it is not indented. Change the first line so it is properly indented and tell students that it still is not a paragraph. If no one else volunteers information, proceed to step two.

Step Two: Direct Instruction

Paragraphs are groups of sentences that tell about the same idea, or topic. They are made up of two kinds of sentences: topic sentences and detail sentences. Every paragraph has one and only one topic sentence. It is the sentence that tells us what the rest of the paragraph is about. Most of the time, it is the first sentence. In third grade, we will always start our paragraphs with the topic sentence.

After the topic sentence, there are detail sentences that tell more about the topic sentence. They tell us details. That is why they are called detail sentences. There can be any number of detail sentences in a paragraph; from one to a hundred. As a general rule, your paragraphs should be at least five sentences long.

Step Three: Guided Practice

Distribute lined paper. Write this topic sentence on the board: Puppies are fun to play with. Ask students to copy the sentence on their paper. Remind them to indent. Give them five minutes to write three sentences about the topic sentence. Ask for four or five volunteers to read their favorite sentence. Write the sentences on the board. Review each detail sentence and make sure that it tells about a way that puppies are fun. Erase any sentences that don't fit.

Repeat this exercise with this topic sentence: Trees are important. Monitor each student and underline sentences that don't belong so that they can change them.

Lesson #35: Paragraph Webs

Step One: Direct Instruction

Draw a simple web like the one below on the board. Explain to students that this is the pattern that shows how paragraphs are organized. Write the words "topic sentence" in the middle

bubble. Write the words "detail sentence" in all the bubbles connected to it. The bubbles are connected because the ideas in the detail sentences are connected to the idea in the topic sentence.

The web has two functions. When students read, it will help them organize the information and make it easier to remember. When they write, it will help them plan so that the finished paragraph is organized and easy to understand. Students need to understand both of these functions.

The information that is written in a web is a fact or idea. Do not write them in complete sentences.

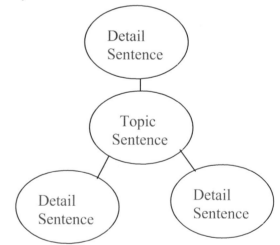

Step Two: Gather Facts

Tell students to listen carefully and try to remember as many facts as they can. Read the information below about starfish. You may use the PowerPoint presentation for Lesson #35 provided at www.WritingandKids.com instead of reading the information.

Then, ask students to share the facts they remember. Record the facts on the board, numbering each one. **Do not write in complete sentences. Record only six facts.**

Starfish

Starfish are not really fish. Starfish do not have bones. They have a skeleton on the outside of their body. They have rows of tube feet for crawling. These animals have a mouth on the bottom of their bodies, in the center. They have no brain. They have spiny skin for protection.

Starfish Facts:

1. Starfish are not fish
2. No bones
3. skeleton on outside
4. rows of tube feet to crawl
5. mouth on bottom
6. no brain
7. spiny skin for protection

Step Three: Web Guided Practice

Distribute the Web to Paragraph page (p. 81) to all students.

Brainstorm some possible topic sentences. Remind them that the topic sentence needs to tell about the whole paragraph, not just one fact. Teachers may also contribute some ideas. The list should look something like this:

I'm going to tell you some facts about starfish.

I learned many things about starfish.

I know about starfish.

Starfish are interesting (cool, fascinating, wonderful, terrible, etc.).

I am writing about starfish.

I'm going to tell you about starfish.

A starfish is a creature that lives in the ocean.

The goal is that students will internalize these topic sentences as templates. If they do that, they will not have to think of a new topic sentence every time they write a paragraph. As they become more sophisticated writers, their topic sentences will become more complex and more unique. For some students this may not happen for several more years.

Ask students to point to the place in the web where they are going to write the topic sentence. Students will choose one of the topic sentences from the list on the board and copy it into the center bubble of their web.

Students should then copy the six facts from the fact list on the board into the six detail sentence bubbles on the web. They should copy them exactly as they are written.

Topic Sentence--On the lines below the web, students will write a paragraph from the information on their web. Students should begin with the topic sentence.   Remind them to indent the topic sentence one index finger's width from the left margin.

Detail Sentences—Now students are going to add detail sentences to their paragraphs. This will require students to add words to each fact to convert them into complete sentences.

Begin with one of the facts. Demonstrate how to add words to turn the fact into a complete sentence. Write the sentence in the paragraph.

Move to the second fact. Ask students to add words to change the fact into a sentence. Ask for volunteers to share their answers.

Repeat this process until the entire paragraph is finished.

This is powerful teaching. Not only are students practicing paragraph writing, but they are gaining experience with correcting sentence structure as well. This exercise also helps build a foundation for note-taking skills that will be needed for report writing in future years.

Step Four: Independent Web Practice

Post the Topic Sentence Templates where students can see them. In addition, distribute a copy of the Topic Sentence Template page (p. 88) to each student. Ask them to keep it in a safe place so that they can refer to it over and over again until they've memorized them.

Topic Sentence Templates

- I'm going to tell you some facts about _____.
- I learned many things about _____.
- I know about _____.
- _____ are interesting (cool, fascinating, wonderful, terrible, etc.).
- I am writing about _____.
- I'm going to tell you about _____.
- A _____ is _(definition)_ .

Tell students to listen carefully and try to remember as many facts as they can. Read the article about crabs (p. 82). Then, ask students to tell the facts they remember.   Record the facts on the board, numbering each one. Do not write in complete sentences. If they can't list at least eight, add facts until there are eight.

Distribute a copy of the Web to Paragraph page (p. 81) to each student. Students should write their topic sentence in the center bubble of their web. They should then choose six facts from the fact list on the board and copy them into the six detail sentence bubbles on the web. They should copy them exactly as they are written.

On the lines below the web, students will write a paragraph from the information on their web. Students should begin with the topic sentence. Remind them to indent the topic sentence.

Students should finish writing all the detail sentences from the facts in the web. This may require them to add words to convert the facts into complete sentences.

Teachers should monitor students carefully until they can copy the facts and write the paragraphs independently with no errors. If there are too many errors, students should re-write the paragraph portion of the assignment.

Lesson #36: Web to Paragraph
Practice Level 2

This lesson will be a repeat of Step Four from Lesson #35. For your

convenience, the steps are listed in a brief form at the end of this lesson.

Post the Topic Sentence Templates where students can see them. In addition, distribute a copy of the Topic Sentence Template page to each student. Ask them to keep it in a safe place so that they can refer to it over and over again until they've memorized them.

Step One: Gather Information

Tell students to listen carefully and try to remember as many facts as they can. Read one of the sea life articles from the Sea Life Articles pages (p.82). Then, ask students to tell the facts they remember. Record the facts on the board, numbering each one. Do not write in complete sentences. If they can't list at least eight, add facts until there are eight.

Step Two: Choose Six Facts

Distribute a copy of the Web to Paragraph page to each student. Students should write their topic sentence in the center bubble of their web. They should then choose six facts from the fact list on the board and copy them into the six detail sentence bubbles on the web. They should copy them exactly as they are written.

Step Three: Write the Paragraph

On the lines below the web, students will write a paragraph from the information on their web. Students should begin with the topic sentence. Remind them to indent the topic sentence. Students should finish writing all the detail sentences from the facts in the web. This may require them to add words to convert the facts into complete sentences.

Teachers should monitor students carefully until they can copy the facts and write the paragraphs independently with no errors. If there are too many errors, students should re-write the paragraph portion of the assignment.

Continue to repeat this lesson until you've used all the articles on the Sea Life Article page (p.82): octopi, sharks, shrimp, jellyfish, and sea anemones. Each exercise will take an entire class period. However, allow extra time to work individually with students who need extra assistance.

These pages can be assembled into a booklet for each student.

Step Summary

1. Post the topic sentence templates.

2. Read the article.

3. Write down at least eight facts on the board.

4. Student will write a topic sentence.

5. Students will copy six facts into the detail sentence bubble.

6. Students will write the paragraph from the web.

Lesson #37: Web to Paragraph
Practice Level 3 (1-2 class periods)

In this lesson, students will write multiple paragraphs from a multiple-paragraph web.

Step One: Direct Instruction

Display the multiple paragraph web #1 shown on page 87. Distribute a copy of this page to each student, along with a page of lined paper.

Ask students to number the topic sentences in web #1. Then number them on the display page.

Beginning with paragraph #1, ask students to write the topic sentence on their paper. Remind them to indent. Ask for a volunteer to share their sentence. Write the sentence on the board or chart paper for the class to see.

Repeat this process with the remaining sentences in paragraph #1.

Step Two: Guided Practice

Students will write paragraph #2. Monitor closely and assist those students who still need help.

Step Three: Independent Practice

Students will look at the second web on p. 87.   Ask students to number the topic sentences.   Students will write the paragraphs from the web independently.

Lesson #38: Web to Paragraph Practice Level 4 (1-2 class periods)

In this lesson, students will write multiple paragraphs from a multiple-paragraph web.

Step One: Direct Instruction

Display Multiple Paragraphs from a Web Practice #3 (p.88). Distribute a copy of this page to each student, along with a page of lined paper.

Ask students to number the topic sentences.   Then number them on the display page.

Beginning with paragraph #1, ask students to write the topic sentence on their paper. Remind them to indent. Ask for a volunteer to share their sentence. Write the sentence on the board or chart paper for the class to see.

Repeat this process with the remaining sentences in paragraph #1.

Step Two: Guided Practice

Students will write paragraph #2. Monitor closely and assist those students who still need help.

Step Three: Independent Practice

Students will look at Web #4. Ask students to number the topic sentences. Students will write the paragraphs from the web independently.

Lesson #39: Topic Sentence Practice

Step One: Direct Instruction

Display the Topic Sentence Demonstration Page (p. 90).

Read the paragraph first.   Ask students if they can tell which sentence tells about all the other sentences. The first sentence is the topic sentence because all the other sentences provide details about the tricks that dogs can do.

Step Two: Guided Practice

Continue to display the Topic Sentence Demonstration Page (p. 90).

Ask students to look at the paragraph and write the topic sentence on paper or white boards. Randomly ask students how they figured out which sentence was the topic sentence.

Repeat this process for the third

paragraph.

For the last group of paragraphs, ask students to find which sentence doesn't belong in the paragraph.

Ask students to explain why they chose that sentence.

Step Three: Independent Practice

Distribute Topic Sentence Practice #1 worksheet (p. 91). Review directions for both parts. Students should be able to complete the worksheet independently.

Lesson #40: More Topic Sentence Practice

Step One: Review the answers for Topic Sentence Practice #1 worksheet.

Step Two: Direct Instruction
Review these ideas:

What is a topic sentence? It is the sentence that all the other sentences. There is a Powerpoint presentation available for this lesson.

Step Three: Guided Practice

Distribute Topic Sentence Practice #2 worksheet (p. 92). Review directions. Complete the first paragraph in each section with students.

Step Four: Independent Practice

Students should be able to complete the remainder of the worksheet independently.

Lesson #41: Writing Paragraphs from Prompts

Step One: Direct Instruction

A Powerpoint presentation is available online that can be used in lieu of Steps One and Two. The topic sentence templates should be available to students during this lesson.

Key Teaching Point: Use a topic sentence template to write a topic sentence every time you're given a prompt.

Not all prompts are of equal difficulty. Some prompts are more difficult because students must take some time to think before they write.

Show students the first prompt pattern and provide a sample of the prompt. Ask students to use one of the topic sentence templates to write a topic sentence. Share answers. Repeat this process with the remaining prompts. Choose one of the prompts and write a complete paragraph.

These **Paragraph Prompt Patterns** are listed here in order from easiest to most difficult.

- 1. Write a paragraph using this topic sentence. (Provide a topic sentence.)
- 2. Write a paragraph about _____. (Provide the topic.)
- 3. Why or how or what? (Ask a question about a given topic.)
- 4. Write about five things you have learned about _____.
- 5. Write a paragraph telling why or how _____.
- 6. Which one and why?
- 7. Tell about _____.
- 8. Explain _____ in detail.

Examples of Actual Prompts

If the class was studying insects, you might use these prompts.

1. Write a paragraph using this topic sentence: Insects are helpful to humans in many ways.

2. Write a paragraph about ants.

3. Why are insects dangerous to humans?

4. Write five things you have learned about insects.

5. Write a paragraph telling how a caterpillar changes into a butterfly.

6. Which insect do you think is the most interesting and why?

7. Tell about termites.

8. Explain in detail how insects protect themselves from their enemies.

Step Two: Guided Practice

Distribute the Answering Paragraph Prompts worksheet (p.86) to each student. Complete Parts A and B on the worksheet one at a time.   Students will share answers.

Step Three: Independent Practice

Students will complete Parts C and D of the Answering Paragraph Prompts worksheet independently.

Step Four: Continued Practice

Continue to assign independent writing assignments that use pattern #1 until most students have mastered it. (Allow at least 3-4 assignments.) Then begin giving prompts using pattern #2.

Repeat this process until students are able to write a satisfactory paragraph using every prompt pattern. Once they've mastered all the patterns, you can vary the pattern for each assignment. This process should continue at least three days per week for the remainder of the school year as part of their independent writing.

Pattern #1

Write a paragraph using this topic sentence: I am going to tell you how to find a word in a dictionary.

Write a paragraph using this topic sentence: I know how to get good grades in school.

Write a paragraph using this topic sentence: I'm writing about the best birthday party I ever had.

Pattern#2

Write a paragraph about frogs.

Write a paragraph about a peanut butter and jelly sandwich.

Write a paragraph about the ocean.

Pattern #3

What are the three kinds of sentences?

What is your favorite book?

Why do you use your five senses when you describe the setting in a story?

Pattern #4

Write five things you have learned about writing a paragraph.

Write about three things that you know about sea animals.

Write about five facts that you know about your city.

Pattern #5

Write a paragraph telling why you should brush your teeth.

Write a paragraph telling how to sharpen a pencil.

Write a paragraph telling why you should do your homework.

Pattern #6

Does a cat or a dog make the best pet? Why?

Should you do your homework with a pencil or a crayon? Why?

Is it better to live in the city or the country? Why?

Pattern #7

Tell about potatoes.

Write about chickens.

Tell about rainbows.

Pattern #8

Explain in detail how you get ready for school in the morning.

Explain in detail what your best friend is like.

Would you like to be an astronaut? Explain your answer in detail.

Web to Paragraph

SEA LIFE ARTICLES

Crabs

A crab is a kind of animal called a crustacean. There are approximately 6,800 kinds of crabs. They belong to the same family or group of animals that includes lobsters and shrimp.

Nearly all crabs live in oceans, but some live in fresh water like lakes and rivers. Some crabs even live on land.

Algae is the crabs' favorite food. They also eat worms and other crustaceans. Most crabs eat dead plants and animals.

Crabs have ten jointed legs. These joints help the legs bend. You have joints on your legs too. Your knees and ankles and hips are joints. Two of the crab's legs have large claws. They use these claws to fight their enemies. They also use them to gather food. If a claw breaks off, the crab will grow a new one.

Crabs have two eyes that are on the end of stalks. This helps the crab see in all directions at once.

Crabs are covered with a thick exoskeleton. This means that instead of having a skeleton inside their body, they have a skeleton on the outside of their body. We usually call the exoskeleton a shell. This shell protects them from their enemies.

Crabs Facts list (teacher use only)
1. 6,800 kinds of crabs
2. Crustacean
3. Same animal family as lobsters and shrimp
4. Ten jointed legs
5. Two legs have claws
6. Use claws to fight and gather food
7. Two eyes on stalks
8. Skeleton outside of their body
9. Shell protects them from enemies
10. Live in oceans, lakes, rivers, on land
11. Eat algae, worms, and other crustaceans

Octopus

Octopuses have very large heads. They are very smart. They have very good brains and can remember and learn things.

An octopus is a mollusk. Octopuses have no skeleton. They're in the same animal family as snails, clams, and oysters.

An octopus has eight arms which are attached to its head. If you look closely at an octopus's arms, you'll see rows of suckers. Octopuses use their suckers to taste things and to hold onto things.
Octopuses live only in salt water. This generally means that octopuses live in oceans. You won't find octopuses in lakes or rivers.

Octopuses are born from eggs. They are about the size of a grain of rice. When they grow up, they'll be 2-3 feet across. Octopuses live only one or two years.

Octopuses hunt for food mostly at night. They eat crabs, lobsters, fish, clams, and mussels. They catch their prey with their arms and bite them with their parrot-like beak.

Octopuses like to live in small holes in shallow water. Sometimes they'll find a hole in a rock. Sometimes they'll dig a den in the dirt. Because they have no skeleton, octopuses can fit into very small spaces. Often they hide their homes with shells.

When an octopus thinks it's in danger, it can squirt out a purplish black ink cloud. This confuses its enemy and gives the octopus a chance to get away.

Octopuses can walk on the ocean floor, but they can also move by pushing water out of their siphon. It makes them "jet" through the water.

Octopus Facts list (teacher use only)
1. Eight arms attached to its head
2. Suckers on arms used to taste and hold things
3. Live in salt water
4. Only live one or two years
5. Grow to be 2-3 feet across
6. Hunt at night
7. Eat lobsters, crabs, clams, mussels, and fish
8. Squirts purple ink cloud to confuse enemies
9. Live in small holes
10. jet through the water using their siphon

Jellyfish

Jellyfish aren't really fish. They're very odd animals that are found in every ocean all over the world. Some live near the surface and some live in the very deepest parts of the ocean. Their bodies look like blobs of clear jelly. Their body is shaped like an umbrella and they have long tentacles that hang from the edge of their bodies.

Some jellyfish have tentacles that are 120 feet long. All jellyfish sting their prey with stinging cells on their tentacles. They use their tentacles to protect themselves and also to catch food. The poison from their sting can be deadly to humans. You have to be very careful not to get stung by a jellyfish.

Jellyfish's bodies are mostly made of water. They have no brains, no stomachs, and no gills. They get oxygen from the water directly through their surface of their bodies.

Jellyfish Facts list (teacher use only)
1. not fish
2. tentacles can be 120 feet long
3. live in every part of the ocean
4. tentacles can sting
5. use tentacles to protect themselves
6. use tentacles to catch food
7. sting can be deadly to humans
8. bodies made mostly of water
9. no brains, stomachs, or gills
10. get oxygen directly through body surface

Sea Anemones

Sea anemones are in the animal family Cnidaria just like jellyfish. Because they're in the same family, they have many things in common. They're called anemones because they look like flowers. Unlike jellyfish, sea anemones attach themselves to solid objects like rocks and stay in one place their entire lives. You can often see them attached to rocks near the beach.

The anemone's mouth is in the center of their body and it's surrounded by tentacles. An anemone can have between 20 and several hundred tentacles. The tentacles can sting their prey. Anemones have no stomach. They pull their prey into their body and digest it there. Sea anemones like to eat fish and crustaceans (like shrimp).

They have no eyes and no brain. They can be as small as ¼ inch or as large as 6 feet across but usually they're between one and three inches across

Sea Anemone Facts list (teacher use only)

1. cnidaria
2. same animal family as jellyfish
3. attach to a solid object
4. mouth surrounded by tentacles
5. tentacles sting prey
6. no stomach
7. eat fish and crustaceans like shrimp
8. no eyes and no brain
9. usually 1-3 inches across
10. 20-several hundred tentacles

Sharks

There are 440 different kinds of sharks. The smallest sharks only grow to be 7 inches long and the longest grow to be 39 feet.

Sharks are known for their sharp teeth. Sharks are continuously losing and growing new teeth. Some sharks may lose and grow 35,000 teeth in their lifetime.

A shark's skeleton is not made of bone like a fish skeleton. It is made of cartilage like your nose and ears.

Most sharks need to constantly swim in order to breathe. If they sleep for too long, they'll sink.

Shark skin is made of tiny, hard, tooth-like scales. These scales make the skin feel like sandpaper. It protects them from their enemies and parasites. It also helps them swim faster.

Most sharks live 20-30 years, but some sharks can live up to 100 years.

Sharks are carnivores, which means they eat meat. Some sharks will eat anything, but most kinds of sharks eat a very particular type of animal and nothing else.

Sharks Facts List (teacher use only)

1. 440 different kinds
2. Size varies from 7 inches to 39 feet
3. Continuously grow and lose teeth
4. Skin is tiny, hard scales
5. Skin feels like sandpaper

6. Most live 20-30 years
7. Some live 100 years
8. Carnivores
9. Need to swim to breathe
10. Skeleton made of cartilage

Shrimp

Shrimp are crustaceans like crabs. There are more than 2,000 kinds of shrimp. They live in both fresh and salt water. They live close to the bottom.

They have a thin exoskeleton which we call a shell. In the water, the shell is colorless. This makes the shrimp hard to see.

Shrimp have five pairs of jointed walking legs. They have five pairs of swimming legs and three pairs of feeding legs. They breathe through gills like fish.

Shrimp are pretty small. They grow from ½ inch to 12 inches long. Depending on the kind of shrimp, they only live from one to six years.

Shrimps are omnivorous. That means they eat both plants and animals. They eat algae along with tiny fish and plankton in the water.

Shrimp Facts List (teacher use only)
1. Crustaceans
2. 2,000 kinds
3. Fresh and salt water
4. Live near the bottom
5. Thin exoskeleton
6. Colorless exoskeleton makes them hard to see
7. ½ inch to 12 inches long
8. Live from 1-6 years
9. 13 pairs of jointed legs
10. Breathe through gills like fish
11. Omnivorous
12. Eat algae, small fish, and plankton

Answering Paragraph Prompts

Name_____

Part A   Write a topic sentence to answer each prompt. You can only use each topic sentence template once.

1.   Write a paragraph about ducks.

   _____

2. Tell about marshmallows.

   _____

3. Explain in detail how to write a paragraph.

   _____

4. Would you like to travel to Mars? Why?

   _____

5. Write a paragraph telling how to make a paper airplane.

   _____

Part B   Choose one of the topic sentences above and write a complete paragraph.

   _____
   _____
   _____
   _____

Part C   Write a topic sentence to answer each prompt. You can only use each topic sentence template once.

6. Write a paragraph telling five things you know about the sun.

   _____

7. What is your favorite summer activity?

   _____

8. Writing a paragraph telling what plants need to grow.

   _____

9. Tell about the moon.

   _____

10. Explain in detail what your teacher looks like.

   _____

Part D   Choose one of the topic sentences above and write a complete paragraph.

   _____
   _____
   _____
   _____

MULTIPLE PARAGRAPHS FROM A WEB #1

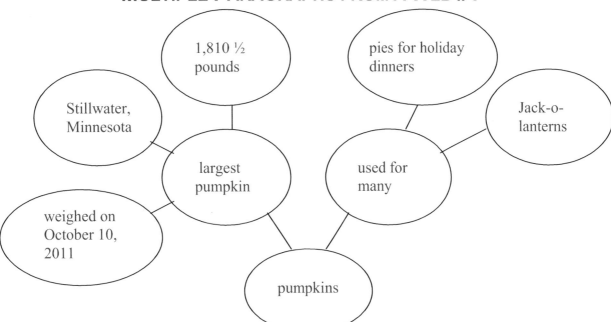

MULTIPLE PARAGRAPHS FROM A WEB #2

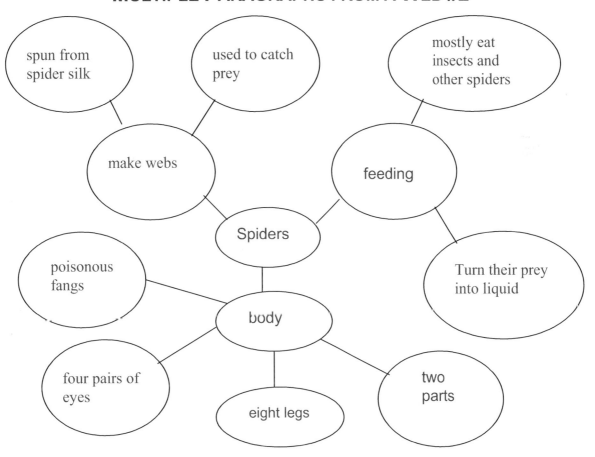

MULTIPLE PARAGRAPHS FROM A WEB #3

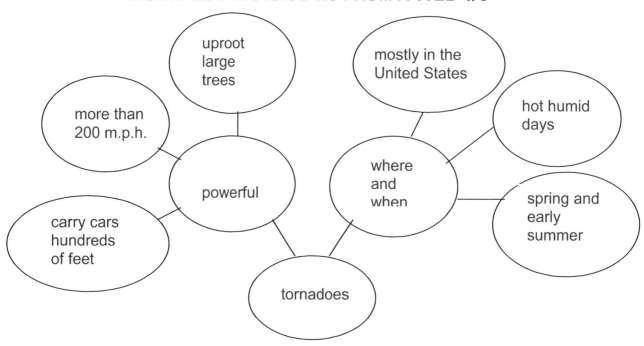

WEB TO MULTIPLE PARAGRAPH PRACTICE #4

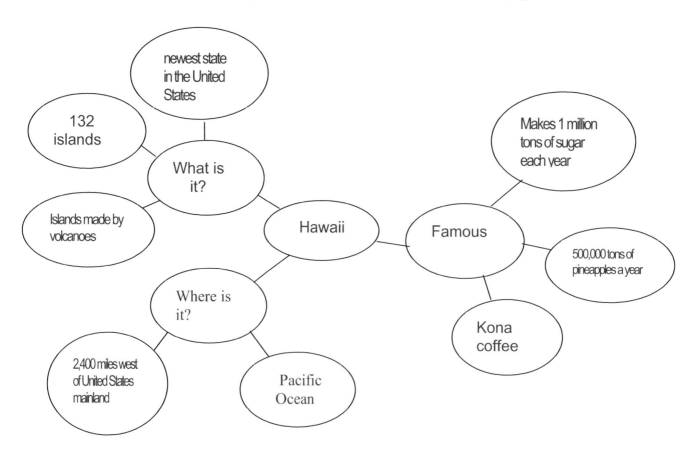

TOPIC SENTENCE TEMPLATES
NAME_____

1. I'm going to tell you some facts about _____.

2. I learned many things about _____.

3. I know about _____.

4. _____ are interesting (cool, fascinating, wonderful, terrible, etc.).

5. I am writing about _____.

6. I'm going to tell you about _____.

7. A _____ is _(definition)_ .

TOPIC SENTENCE DEMONSTRATION PAGE

What is a topic sentence?

A topic sentence is the sentence that tells the main idea of a paragraph.

Paragraph #1

Dogs can do lots of tricks. Some dogs can catch frisbees. Some dogs will shake hands. Many dogs will sit and stay when they're told. Many dogs will chase a ball and bring it back.

Paragraph #2

It's fun to swing on the swings and slide down the slide. You can play on the monkey bars. You can climb the rope ladder. There are many things to do at the playground.

Paragraph #3

You can slurp the noodles. You can wind the noodles on your fork. Spaghetti is fun to eat. You can roll the meatballs across the table.

What is a detail sentence?

A detail sentence is a sentence that tells more information about the topic sentence.

Paragraph #4

The Mississippi River is the longest river in the United States. It is 2,348 miles long. I'm going to tell you about the Mississippi River. The river starts in Lake Itasca in Minnesota and ends in Louisiana. At its widest point, it's 4,500 feet wide. Ships carry many products up and down the river.

Paragraph #5

My grandmother likes to make quilts. She stitches all the pieces together in wonderful patterns. People buy her quilts. She buys many different kinds of fabric to make the patterns. She sits and sews all day.

Paragraph #6

I know some facts about the Grand Canyon. The Colorado River flows through it. In some places, it's a mile deep. It's fun to vacation in summer. It took 3-6 million years to form.

Paragraph #7

I'm going to tell you about bees. Bees are flying insects. They are famous for making honey and beeswax. They have a long tongue that helps them get nectar from flowers. Ants are insects too.

Topic Sentence Worksheet #1
Name_____

A. Directions: Underline the topic sentence in each paragraph below. Remember that the topic sentence must talk about all of the other sentences in the paragraph.

1. The crust is nice and chewy. Pizza is the best food. Two slices will make you full. The cheese melts in your mouth. You can make it with lots of different things on top.	2. Mix flour and eggs in a big mixing bowl. Stir in sugar and baking powder. Put twelve spoonfuls on a cookie pan and put them in the oven. Making cookies is easy.
3. Raptors are birds that hunt prey. They have good eyes that help them see small animals from far away. Raptors have sharp talons and hooked beaks that help them tear meat. Raptors fly fast to catch prey that is running.	4. There are more kinds of reptiles in the Amazon Jungle than anywhere else. Many animals live in the jungle. Parrots and hummingbirds fly in the jungle. Piranha and catfish swim in the rivers. There are many, many different kinds of ants.

B. **Directions:** In the following paragraphs, cross out the sentence that does not belong.

5. Deserts are very hot. It can be 120 degrees in the daytime. If you walk on the hot ground, you can burn your feet. You will sweat and the sun can burn your skin. Cacti grow in the desert.	6. Farmers grow many things on their farms. They have to get up very early in the morning. They raise animals like cows, horses, chickens, and pigs. Some farmers also grow corn, wheat, potatoes, and cotton. They also grow many kinds of fruit like peaches, apples, pears, and apricots.
7. Spiders are the only animals that can spin webs. Spiders have eight eyes. They have special spinnercts on their body that make the silk. They use the webs to catch their food. Spider webs are stronger than steel.	8. We use the roots of many plants for food. Carrots, beets, and sweet potatoes are actually the roots of the plant. Root plants are very good for you. Long ago, people used roots to dye their clothes different colors. Roots contain starch that gives you energy when you eat it.

Topic Sentence Worksheet #2
Name_____

A. **Directions:** Underline the topic sentence in each paragraph below. Remember that the topic sentence must talk about all of the other sentences in the paragraph.

1. North America and South America are two continents. The Earth has seven continents. Australia is the only continent that is an island. Antarctica is a continent that is at the South Pole. The continents of Europe and Asia are right next to each other. The Sahara Desert is found on the continent of Africa.	2. Raisins are made from grapes. The grapes are picked when they are ripe and sweet. Most raisins are made from green grapes. The grapes are placed on paper in the vineyard so the sun can dry them. When they dry, they turn black and wrinkly.
3. You must have a fishing pole to catch a fish. You don't need a boat. Put some bait on your hook and throw it in the water. Reel the fish in when it bites. It is easy to catch a fish.	4. The leaves turn orange, red, yellow, and brown. Some people travel a long way to see the trees changing colors. The trees are shutting down the food making factories in their leaves. The leaves of some trees change color in autumn. The trees are getting ready to rest during the winter.

B. **Directions:** In the following paragraphs, cross out the sentence that does not belong.

5. Pumpkins come in many sizes. They usually weigh between nine and eighteen pounds. Pumpkins are a kind of squash. Some pumpkins weigh less than a pound. The largest pumpkin recorded weighed an unbelievable 1,810 pounds.	6. Many animals hibernate in the winter. Hibernating saves energy during the winter months. Animals that hibernate sleep all winter and don't eat. During the fall, the animals eat extra food so that they can stay alive while they hibernate.
6. Christopher Columbus sailed to America in 1492. He sailed with three ships named the Nina, the Pinta, and the Santa Maria. It took Christopher Columbus 70 days to reach America. Christopher Columbus had two sons named Diego and Fernando. The trip was paid for by Queen Isabella of Portugal.	7. Milk is good for you. It comes with chocolate and strawberry flavor. It contains protein which helps keep your muscles and other organs healthy. The calcium in milk helps your bones and teeth grow strong. The vitamins in milk keep you from getting sick.

CONCEPT #4: PARAGRAPH WRITING
PART 2: PARAGRAPH TO WEB

Foundation Information

Once students have learned how to write a paragraph from a web, they must learn the reverse process. They must learn to create a web from a paragraph. Both of these steps are essential in order for students to internalize the web pattern. Once this occurs, the web becomes an integral part of how they understand all non-fiction text. Although the time will come when students will no longer physically write information into a web, their brains will continue to seek out the topic sentence and the details in the material they read, increasing their ability to comprehend and retain the information.

and the detail sentences.

Step Two: Guided Practice

Students will write the topic sentence on the first line.

Beginning with the first fact, students will write a complete detail sentence using that fact. Ask for volunteers to share their sentences.

Repeat this process for the second fact.

Step Three: Independent Practice

Students will complete the remainder of the paragraph using the facts provided.

Lesson #42: Web to Paragraph Review

Step One: Direct Instruction

Show the Web to Paragraph Review (p. 95) on an overhead projector or smart board. Distribute a copy of the page for each student.

Review the structure of a paragraph web with students. With students' help, locate the topic sentence

Lesson #43: Paragraph to Web-- Direct Instruction and Guided Practice

Step One: Tell students that you are going to reverse the process of writing a paragraph from a web. This time they are going to make a web from a paragraph.

Step Two: Distribute the Paragraph to Web Practice #1 worksheet (p. 96).

Complete this worksheet together as a class. Ask students to locate the topic sentence. Students should underline only the most important words in the sentence. Tell them they want to find the fact in the sentence.

EXAMPLES:

Topic Sentence: I'm going to tell you some facts about <u>squid</u>.

Fact: Squid

(The rest of the sentence doesn't provide any information)

Detail Sentence: The sun is a <u>medium-sized star.</u>

Fact: medium-sized star

(The word star doesn't need to be underlined because it would be included in the topic sentence.)

Detail Sentence: The Hopi Indians build homes called pueblos.

Fact: homes called pueblos

(The words *Hopi Indians* don't need to be underlined because they would be included in the topic sentence.)

As a class, put the important words into the shortest possible phrase that makes sense. Students usually grasp this idea quickly, as they have had some practice during the writing of their initial paragraphs. Students will then write the phrase in the center of the web.

Proceed to the first detail sentence. Once again, direct students to underline the most important words. Put the words into a short phrase. Write the phrase in one of the detail sentence bubbles. Repeat these steps with the remaining detail sentences until the whole paragraph has been "webbed".

Lesson #44: Paragraph to Web-- **Independent Practice**

Distribute the Paragraph to Web Practice #2 worksheet (p. 97). Allow students to web the paragraph independently. Monitor closely and provide assistance on an individual basis as necessary.

Web to Paragraph Review

Name_____

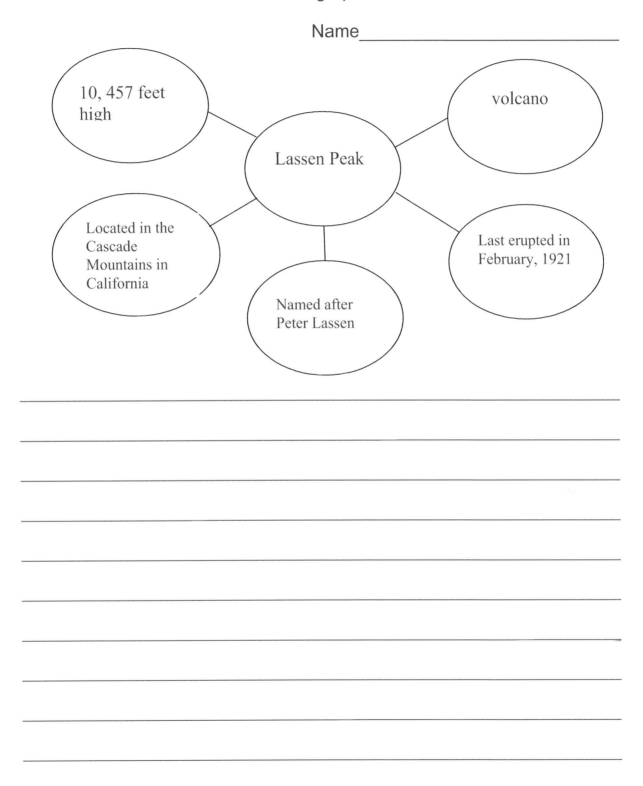

_____

_____

_____

_____

_____

_____

_____

_____

_____

Paragraph to Web Practice #1

Name_____

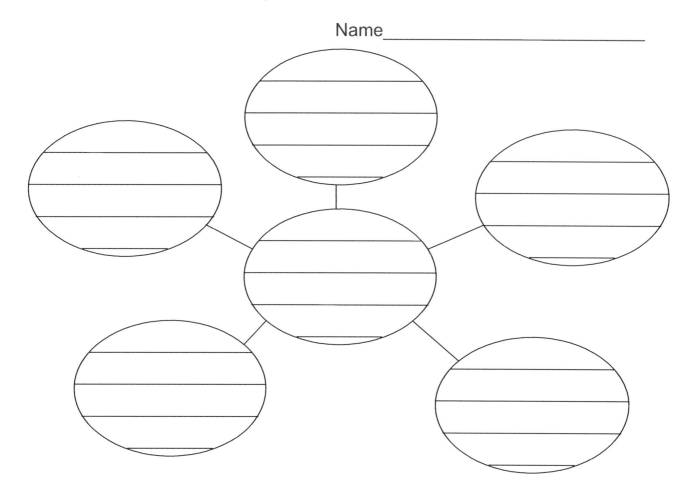

I'm going to tell you five facts about Koalas. Koalas live on the continent of Australia. They have gray or brown fur on their back and white fur on their bellies. They are usually nocturnal animals that are awake during the night. They sleep all day in the forks of eucalyptus trees. They eat the leaves of the trees.

Paragraph to Web Practice #2
Name _____

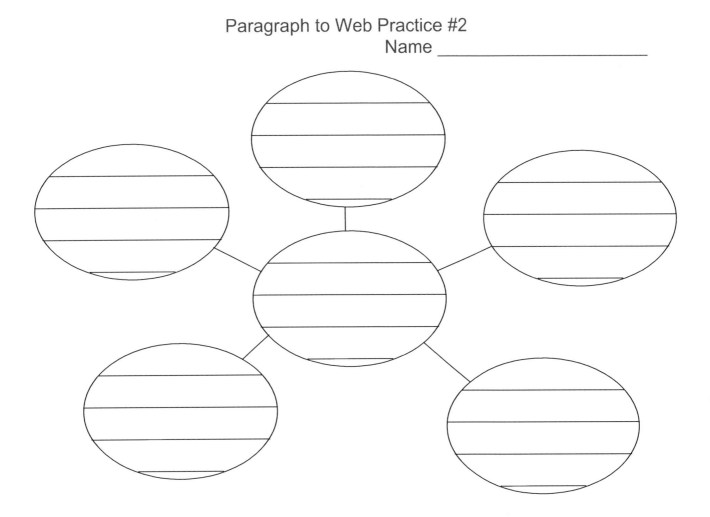

Peanut butter can be used to make many wonderful things. It can be spread on bread to make a sandwich. I love to mix it into dough and bake it into peanut butter cookies. It can also be made into delicious peanut butter cups that are covered in chocolate. It can be turned into peanut butter ice cream. Many people like to eat peanut butter when it's spread on celery stalks.

CONCEPT #4: PARAGRAPH WRITING
PART 3: MULTIPLE PARAGRAPH WEBS

The next step in writing non-fiction is to expand from a single paragraph to multiple paragraphs. As with a single paragraph, it is imperative that students learn the pattern, not just the process.

Lesson #45: Multiple Paragraph Patterns

Practice Level 1

Step One: Direct Instruction

On the chalkboard or overhead, write the following:

Two paragraphs

One paragraph has two detail sentences

One paragraph has three detail sentences

With students' help, begin by drawing a web o the first paragraph as shown below.

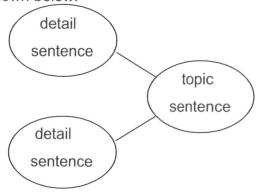

With students' help, draw a web of the second paragraph next to the first so that the illustration looks like the one below.

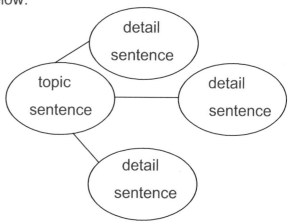

When a person writes more than one paragraph about the same subject, the paragraph webs are connected by the subject. Add a bubble between the two topic sentences. Write "subject" in the bubble and connect the bubble to each topic sentence.

Step Two: Guided Practice

Distribute blank white paper. Students will fold the paper in half, creating a horizontal line. On the chalkboard write:

Two paragraphs

One paragraph has three details

One paragraph has four details

Ask students to draw this web on the top half of their paper. Students will not write actual facts, only the words "topic sentence", "detail sentence", and "subject". Provide assistance as needed.

On the chalkboard, write:

Four paragraphs

One paragraph has two details

Two paragraphs have three details

One paragraph has four details

Students will draw this web on the bottom half of their paper.   Provide assistance as needed.

Step Three: Independent practice

Student will complete the Multiple Paragraph Web Patterns #1 worksheet (p. 103) independently.

Lesson #46: Multiple Paragraph Web Patterns Practice Level 2

Step One: Check for Understanding

Divide students into four teams. Assign one of the webs from Multiple Paragraph Web Patterns #1 worksheet to each team. The team will work together to re-create their web on a large piece of chart paper. Students will share their results with the rest of the class. Students

will check their worksheets against the large version. Teachers should monitor carefully to make sure all students understand the webbing process.

Step Two: Assign the Multiple Paragraph Web Patterns #2 worksheet (p.104). Students will complete this independently.

Lesson #47: Multiple Paragraph Web Patterns Practice Level 3

Step One: Check for Understanding

Correct Multiple Paragraph Web Patterns #2 together as a class.

Step Two: Guided Practice

Assign Multiple Paragraph Web Patterns #3 worksheet (p.105). Students will complete this assignment independently. Teachers should monitor carefully and work individually with students who need continued instruction.

Step Three: Independent Practice

Assign Multiple Paragraph Web Patterns #4 worksheet (p. 106). Students will complete this assignment independently.

Lesson #48: Multiple Paragraph Webs—Practice Level 1 (3-4 class periods)

Step One: Direct Instruction

Distribute a copy of the Multiple

Paragraph Web Practice #1 (p. 107) and one piece of blank 12" x 18"construction paper to each student.

Ask students to number the paragraphs. Then ask students to tell how many topic sentences there are.

On the construction paper, ask students to draw a title bubble in the center and write "Title" in it. Ask them to draw one bubble for each topic sentence and draw a line connecting them to the Title bubble. They should write "Topic Sentence" in each bubble.

Together, count the number of detail sentences in the first paragraph. Draw the appropriate number of detail sentence bubbles and draw a line connecting them to one of the topic sentence bubble. Students should write "Detail Sentence" in each of the bubbles.

Continue this process with the remaining paragraphs.

Step Two: Guided Practice with full support

The guided practice in this lesson will be completing in several steps. In the first step, the teacher will provide complete support. In each succeeding step, the teacher will bring the students one step closer to independence.

Distribute one page of web bubbles (p.109), scissors, and glue to each student.

Students will begin by reading the first paragraph together. Students will write the title in one of the bubbles. They will then cut the bubble out and glue it in the center of the piece of construction paper.

Next, direct students to underline the most important words in the topic sentence of the first paragraph. Tell them how many words they should underline. After giving them a few minutes, underline the words for them on your smart board or write them on the board.

Students will write the words in one of the bubbles, cut it out, and glue it to the paper. Then a line should be drawn connecting it to the bubble containing the title. Repeat the process with the detail sentences of the first paragraph.

As students do this on their paper, the teacher can draw the corresponding web on the board or use the Multiple Paragraph Web#1 PowerPoint presentation.

Step Two: Guided Practice with less support

Proceed to the second paragraph.

Direct students to underline the most important words in the topic sentence. This time, don't tell them how many words they should underline. Check answers together. Students will write them in a bubble.

Demonstrate where the bubble should be placed on the paper by adding it to your web or using the PowerPoint presentation. Monitor students to make sure they connect it to the title bubble.

Students should then place the bubble on the construction paper in the correct place and draw the connecting line.

As students proceed to the detail sentences, ask them to place the bubbles where they think they should be placed. Monitor closely to make sure that they are connected to the topic sentence bubble.

Step Three: Guided Practice with even less support

In this paragraph, students will read the entire paragraph and underline the important details in every sentence of the paragraph. Check and correct each student individually as they finish.

Students may then write the bubbles and cut and paste them in the appropriate location on the paper.

Provide continued assistance to those students who need it.

Point out the connection between the initial multiple paragraph web pattern worksheets that they have completed and the pattern of the current assignment.

At the end of this lesson, save several student samples to use for demonstration purposes in Lesson #49.

Lesson #49: Multiple Paragraph Webs—Practice Level 2 (2-3 class periods)

Step One: Direct Instruction

Distribute a copy of the Multiple Paragraph Web Practice #2 (p. 107) and one piece of blank 12" x 18" construction paper to each student.

Ask students to number the paragraphs. Then ask students to tell how many topic sentences there are.

Show them samples of student work from Lesson #48 so they can remember what the finished product will look like.

On the construction paper, ask students to draw a title bubble and write "Title" in it. Ask them to draw the pattern for their web using bubbles that say only "topic sentence" and "detail sentence". Monitor closely and provide assistance for those students who still need help.

Step Two: Guided Practice

Distribute one page of web bubbles (p.108), scissors, and glue to each student.

Students will use the back side of the construction paper used in Step One. Using the process from Lesson #48, complete the Title and the first paragraph as a class. Students will underline the important words in each sentence and write them on one of the bubbles on the Web Bubble page.   They will cut the bubble out and glue it in the correct place on their paper.

Step Three: Independent Practice

Students should be able to complete the remaining paragraphs independently.   Monitor and provide support as needed.

Save several student papers to use as exemplars for Lesson #50.

Lesson #50: Multiple Paragraph Webs—Practice Level 3

This lesson will be done twice. The first time, use Multiple Paragraph Web Practice #3. The second time, use #4.

Step One: Direct Instruction

Review the steps for creating a web from a paragraph.

1. Find and underline the important words.
2. Write the words in a bubble.
3. Cut out the bubble and glue it in the correct place on the paper.
4. Draw a line connecting detail sentences to topic sentences so that they create a web.

Step Two: Guided Practice

Distribute Multiple Paragraph Web Practice #3 or #4 (p. 108), one page of blank 9" x 12" construction paper, one page of web bubbles (p.109), scissors, and glue to each student.

Using the process from Lesson #48, complete the Title and the first paragraph as a class.

Step Three: Independent Practice

Students should be able to complete the remaining paragraphs independently.   Monitor and provide support as needed.

Multiple Paragraph Web Patterns #1
Name_____

Directions: Draw a web that shows the paragraphs described at the bottom of each box. Write "topic sentence" and "detail sentence" only in your bubbles. In each box, outline each paragraph's bubbles with a different color.

3 paragraphs 1 paragraph has two detail sentences 2 paragraphs have three detail sentences	3 paragraphs 2 paragraphs have two detail sentences 1 paragraph has four detail sentences
4 paragraphs 1 paragraph has 2 detail sentences 2 paragraphs have 3 detail sentences 1 paragraph has 4 detail sentences	2 paragraphs 1 paragraph has 3 detail sentences 1 paragraph has 4 detail sentences

Multiple Paragraph Web Patterns #2
Name_____

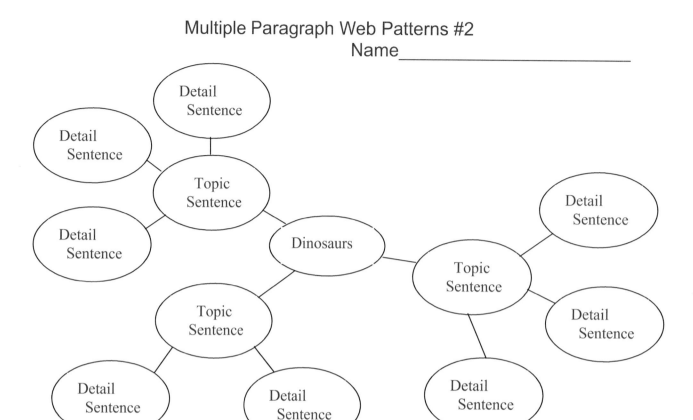

1. How many paragraphs are shown above? _____

2. How do you know? _____

_____

3. How many paragraphs have three detail sentences? _____

4. What is the title of these paragraphs? _____

5. Outline the bubbles above. Use a different color for each paragraph.

6. In the space below, draw a web showing two paragraphs about spiders. One paragraph will have three detail sentences and one paragraph will have four detail sentences. Write the words "topic sentence" and "detail sentence" and the title only in the bubbles.

Multiple Paragraph Web Patterns #3
Name_____

Directions: Draw a web that shows the paragraphs described at the bottom of each box. Write "topic sentence" and "detail sentence" only in your bubbles. In each box, outline each paragraph's bubbles with a different color.

2 paragraphs
1 paragraph has four detail sentences
1 paragraph has two detail sentences

3 paragraphs
2 paragraphs have two detail sentences
1 paragraph has three detail sentences

4 paragraphs
1 paragraph has 3 detail sentences
2 paragraphs have 2 detail sentences
1 paragraph has 4 detail sentences

3 paragraphs
2 paragraphs have 3 detail sentences
1 paragraph has 2 detail sentences

Multiple Paragraph Web Patterns #4

Name_____

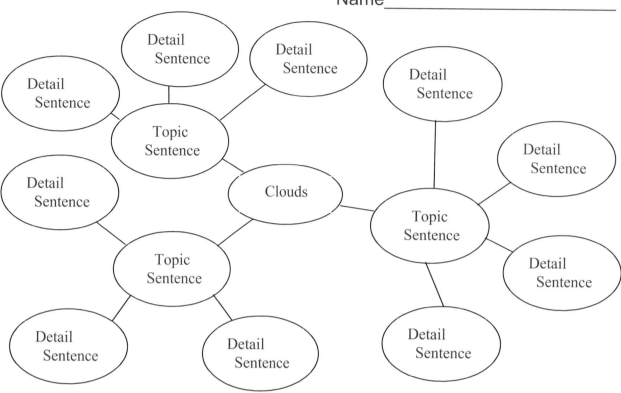

1. How many paragraphs are shown above? _____

2. How do you know? _____

_____

3. How many paragraphs have three detail sentences? _____

4. What is the title of these paragraphs? _____

5. Outline the bubbles above. Use a different color for each paragraph.

6. In the space below, draw a web showing three paragraphs about roses. Two paragraphs will have two detail sentences and one paragraph will have three detail sentences. Write the words "topic sentence" and "detail sentence" and the title only in the bubbles.

MULTIPLE PARAGRAPH TO WEB PRACTICE #1

Disneyland

The original Disneyland Park is located in Anaheim, California. It opened on July 18, 1955. It celebrated its fiftieth anniversary in 2005. It was built by Walt Disney.

You can meet your favorite Disney characters. You can get your picture taken with them. They will also sign your photo book. The characters will give you a big hug. You can even eat dinner with them.

There are many fun things to do in Disneyland. You can visit Sleeping Beauty's castle. There are many roller coasters to ride on. At the end of the night, you can watch a magnificent fireworks display.

MULTIPLE PARAGRAPH TO WEB PRACTICE #2

Spaghetti

Spaghetti is the name for long thin noodles. The noodles are only made of flour and water. The original spaghetti noodles were 20 inches long. Most spaghetti today is only 12 inches long. The noodles are boiled in water.   The noodles are cooked until they're soft on the outside and chewy on the inside.

Spaghetti was invented in Italy, a country by the Mediterranean Sea. It was invented nearly a thousand years ago. When spaghetti was originally made, the noodles were seasoned with butter, raisins, and spices. It was not until around 1840 that spaghetti was eaten with tomato sauce.

The world record for largest bowl of spaghetti was made in March 2010. It was made by a restaurant in Garden Grove, California. The restaurant successfully cooked more than 13,780 pounds of pasta. There was so much pasta, they had to make it in a swimming pool.

MULTIPLE PARAGRAPH TO WEB PRACTICE #3
Autumn

I know about autumn. Autumn is the season of the year right before winter. It usually includes the months of September, October, and November.

Many things change during autumn. The weather gets cooler. The days get shorter and the nights get longer. The leaves of the trees begin to turn colors.

Autumn is harvest time. Peaches, apples, and pumpkins are picked. The food is sold to stores or stored for winter. Many people celebrate the harvest with parties and feasts.

MULTIPLE PARAGRAPH TO WEB PRACTICE #4
Wool

I'm going to tell you where wool comes from. Wool comes from several animals. Most wool comes from sheep. Alpaca wool comes from alpacas. Cashmere wool comes from wool grown on cashmere goats.

Many things are made from wool. It is used in blankets, clothing, and rugs. It is a good cloth to use for coats, hats, and gloves. Many people like to wear wool socks.

I'm going to tell you some facts about wool cloth. Wool cloth is easy to clean. It doesn't get wrinkled very easily. It can keep a person very warm in cold weather.

I'm going to tell you the five steps people use to make wool cloth. First, the wool must be sheared (cut) from the sheep. Next, workers remove stained and damaged wool. Third, the wool is cleaned and untangled. Fourth, the wool is spun into yarn. Finally, the yarn is woven or knitted into cloth.

Web Bubbles

CONCEPT #5: VENN DIAGRAMS

Venn Diagram Key Teaching Points

A Venn diagram is a non-fiction writing tool made from two intersecting circles.

B. It is used when comparing and contrasting two things.

C. Students don't need to write complete sentences.

Look carefully at the Model Venn Diagram on page 115. There are instructions on it which will make the Venn diagram a more efficient planning tool. Look carefully at how the facts are numbered. Notice that each new fact begins on a new line. This is important because the Venn diagram needs to be clear and easy to follow when it is finished. Make sure that students write the topic below each circle.

Always check the students' Venn diagrams before asking them to write the paragraphs.

Lesson #51: Venn Diagram--Direct Instruction (2 class periods)

Step One: Direct Instruction

Complete a Venn diagram comparing ants and bees with students' input.

Draw a large Venn diagram using your chalkboard, overhead projector, or chart paper. In addition, the one in this book can be used on your smart board (p. 114). Teach students about the Venn diagram using the key teaching points.

Under the circle on the left side, write ants. Under the circle on the right side, write bees.

Ask students to share some ways in which ants and bees are the same. In the center portion where the two circles intersect, write three students' answers. Because the Venn diagram is a planning tool like a web, do not write complete sentences.

Sample answers may look like this:
1. insects
2. six legs
3. three body parts

Ask students to tell the class some ways in which ants and bees are different. When writing differences, encourage students to write on both sides simultaneously. For example, on the first line on the left side of the circle labeled ants, the students might write: crawl on the ground. They should then go to the first line on the right side and write about how bees move. Discourage students from simply writing: don't crawl on the ground. Although it's correct, their writing will be better if they learn to give more details and it never hurts to promote a higher level of thinking. "Fly in the air" provides more information and is therefore a much better answer. Ask students to help find three differences between ants and bees.

Step Two: Direct Instruction

Write two paragraphs comparing ants and bees using students' help.

Tell students that the Venn diagram is the plan for writing two paragraphs. One paragraph will be about how ants and bees are the same. One paragraph will be about how ants and bees are different.

Begin with the "same" section of the Venn diagram. Ask students to volunteer to form a topic sentence that tells how ants and bees are the same.

Examples:

- I'm going to tell you how ants and bees are the same.
- I know how ants and bees are the same.
- I'm writing about how ants and

bees are the same.

Write the topic sentence on the chalkboard or smart board. (Ideally, this would be written on chart paper and hung in the room so that students could use it as an example during future assignments.)

With students' help, write a detail sentence for each fact in the "same" section of the Venn diagram.

Example:

Ants and bees are insects. They both have six legs. Ants and bees have six body parts.

The two "difference" portions of the Venn diagram work together to form the second paragraph. Ask the students to suggest a topic sentence for the second paragraph.

Examples:

- Ants and bees are different.
- I can name several differences between ants and bees.

Write the topic sentence on your chalkboard, smart board, overhead projector, or chart paper. Remind students that they must begin the second paragraph on a new line and indent the first sentence. Combine fact #1 about ants and fact #1 about bees into a single sentence.

Example: Ants walk on the ground. Bees can fly. These sentences become: Ants walk on the ground, but bees fly.

Continue with the other two detail sentences.

Lesson #52: Venn Diagram

Practice Level 1 (two-three class periods)

Step One: The Venn Diagram

Distribute a blank copy of the Venn diagram to each student (p. 114). Review the locations of the "same" and "different" portions of the diagram. Students should be able to point to each section. Students should label the sections "same" and "different".

Remind students that each new fact should begin on a new line and be numbered separately.

Students must remember that they should only be writing facts, not entire sentences on the diagram. (As students become more adept at using the Venn diagram as a planning tool, they will begin to shorten their entries.)

Choose a single topic from the Beginning Topics List so that every student is writing about the same topic.

Students should be allowed to work together and share ideas during this initial phase. Most students will need a lot of assistance. Monitor continuously to make sure that students are following the format.

Step Two: Correct the Errors

Collect the diagrams. Correct spelling and format mistakes and return them to the students. Students will recopy the diagram correctly.

Step Three: Write the Paragraphs

Students will then write two paragraphs from the Venn diagram with teacher supervision. Edit any mistakes and ask students to write a final draft.

Beginning Topics List:
knives and scissors
cats and dogs
milk and water
apples and oranges

Lesson #53: Venn Diagrams

Practice Level 2 (3-4 class periods)

Assign a single topic to the entire class. Teachers may want to use the Sea Life paragraphs that students wrote in the previous lessons. Teachers could choose two sea animals that students have already studied.

Distribute a Venn diagram for each student. Students should be able to complete the Venn diagram independently. Check the Venn diagrams and ask students to recopy (if necessary) before allowing them to write the paragraphs. Once the Venn diagram has been checked, students should then write the accompanying paragraphs with minimal teacher assistance. Allow at least two class periods to complete this process.

It is not advisable to send this as a homework assignment until the students have done several Venn diagram assignments independently under teacher supervision.

Lesson #54: Venn Diagram

Practice Level 3 (3-4 class periods)

Students will complete a Venn diagram using one of the curriculum specific topics. Choose a topic that the class is currently studying. The first time (and maybe even the second time) that students do this assignment, check the Venn diagrams before allowing students to proceed with the paragraphs. The first curriculum-specific Venn diagram assignment should be completed entirely in class.

Curriculum-specific Topic Suggestions

- choose two planets
- choose two Indian tribes
- choose two rocks of different origins (igneous, sedimentary, metamorphic)
- choose two dinosaurs
- the Underground Railroad and a real railroad
- covered wagons and cars
- oceans and lakes
- mountains and mesas
- choose two books
- choose two characters from a book
- choose two countries

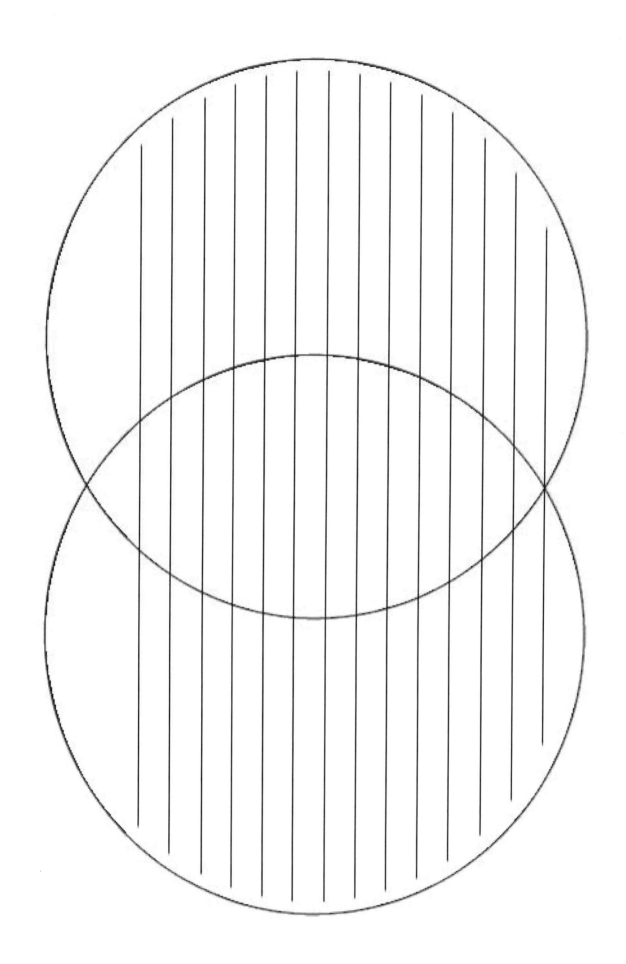

Sample Venn Diagram with Teacher Notes

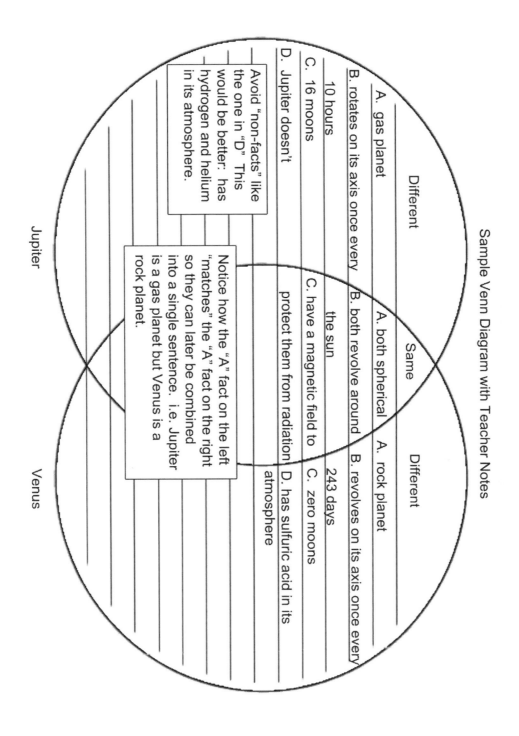

Jupiter

Venus

Different

A. gas planet

B. rotates on its axis once every
10 hours

C. 16 moons

D. Jupiter doesn't

Avoid "non-facts" like
the one in "D." This
would be better: has
hydrogen and helium
in its atmosphere.

Same

A. both spherical

B. both revolve around
the sun

C. have a magnetic field to
protect them from radiation

Different

A. rock planet

B. revolves on its axis once every
243 days

C. zero moons

D. has sulfuric acid in its
atmosphere

Notice how the "A" fact on the left
"matches" the "A" fact on the right
so they can later be combined
into a single sentence. i.e. Jupiter
is a gas planet but Venus is a
rock planet.

CONCEPT #6: WRITING LETTERS

Foundation Information

The letter writing skills that students are required to know in third grade are entirely about the letter format and not about the content. Therefore, once students have mastered the format, you can help them review the format by assigning letters that contain content related to other subjects.

For example, if the class is studying rocks, the teacher could ask students to write a letter to their best friend telling him or her how igneous, sedimentary and metamorphic rocks are made. If the class is studying frogs, the teacher could ask students to write a letter to their Grandma or Grandpa telling them about the life cycle of a frog.

Lesson #55: Letter Writing—the Return Address

Step One: Direct Instruction

Students will begin learning the letter format by learning the return address format. Students make more mistakes on this part of a letter than any other.

Show the Return Address Demonstration Page (p. 118) so that students can view it.

Demonstrate the correct format of the return address by completing #1 while students watch. Be sure to point out where each piece of information should be

placed, and how the address and date should be punctuated.

Step Two: Guided Practice

Use the remaining problems on the Return Address Demonstration Page to allow students to practice with the teacher until they're ready to proceed independently. This can be done using white boards, an individual copy of the demonstration page, or a sheet of paper.

Step Three: Independent Practice

Distribute the Return Address Worksheet (p. 119). Students should be able to complete the worksheet independently.

Lesson #56: Introduction to Letter Writing (2 class periods)

Step One: Direct Instruction

Distribute a copy of the Letter Writing Template page (p. 120) to each student. Place a large copy at the front of the class.

On the large copy, identify the parts of the letter: Heading, Greeting, Body, Closing. Write the names next to the correct location.

Next, as you point to each part and chant them to the children's tune of "Head and Shoulders, Knees, and Toes". Our new version goes like this:

Letter Parts Chant
Heading, Greeting, Body, Close, Body, Close.
Heading, Greeting, Body, Close, Body, Close
Writing Letters—That is how it goes.
Heading, Greeting, Body, Close, Body, Close.

Ask students to sing it with you and point to the correct letter part on their paper with their index finger. Do it several times, increasing speed each time.

Then hide the large copy at the front and call out the parts in a random order and ask students to point to each part.

Next, display the finished sample letter provided (p. 121). Point out how each section is punctuated.

Step Two: Guided Practice

On the Letter Writing Template, students will write a letter to their teacher telling her what they would like to study in class this year. Allow students to view the sample letter as they write. Monitor and provide assistance as needed.

Step Three: Independent Practice

Distribute a new copy of the Letter Writing Template (p.120) for each student. Before beginning, sing the Letter Parts Chant with students again and ask them to point to the correct parts of the letter as they sing.

Ask students to write a letter to a relative telling them about their favorite sport. Students should be able to complete this assignment independently.

They should not be able to view the sample letter as they write.

Lesson #57: Letter Writing— Practice Level 2

Step One: Direct Instruction

Briefly review the parts of a letter by singing the Letter Parts Chant and asking students to point to the correct parts of the letter as they sing.

Place the finished letter where students can refer to it if they need to.

Step Two: Guided Practice

This time when students write their letter, they'll use a piece of standard-size, lined paper instead of the Letter Writing Template.

Choose a curriculum-related topic for students to write about. Monitor and provide assistance as they write.

Step Three: Guided Practice

Repeat the directions for Step Two, but allow students to work independently.

Return Address Demonstration Page

1.Dora lives in Aspen, Colorado (CO), 81611. She lives at 775 Mockingbird Lane.

_____

_____

_____

2. Brandon lives at 82376 E. Frost St. in Detroit, Michigan (MI),48217.

_____

_____

_____

3. John lives in Portland, Oregon(OR), 97213, at 5221 Spruce Drive.

_____

_____

_____

4.Sarah lives at 90887 N. Franklin Ave. in Wheeling, West Virginia (WV), 26003.

_____

_____

_____

5.Olivia lives in Boston, Massachusetts(MA), 02124, at 5 Autumn Court.

_____

_____

_____

Return Address

Name_____

1.Cindy lives in Memphis, Tennessee (TN), 35701. She lives at 354 Pine Street

_____

_____

_____

2. Gustavo lives at 233 Greentree Ave. in Madera, California (CA), 93637.

_____

_____

_____

3. Sophie lives in Phoenix, Arizona (AZ), 85002. She lives at 4909 N. Elm St.

_____

_____

_____

4.Jason lives in West Ely, Missouri (MO) 63401 at 56 Smithview Lane.

_____

_____

_____

5.Ashley lives in Athens, Georgia (GA) 30609 at 901 E. River Dr.

_____

_____

_____

6.Jeremy lives at 8760 W. Fifth St. in Haverhill, Florida (FL), 33415.

_____

_____

_____

7.Hailey lives at 755 Oxford Ave. in Auburn, California (CA),95603.

_____

_____

_____

Letter Writing Template

_____

_____

_____

_____

_____

_____

_____

_____

_____

_____

_____

_____

_____

_____

_____

9065 W. Emerald Ave.
Waterbury, CT 06703
August 5, 2011

Dear Francis,

    I went to the beach on Saturday to collect shells. I collected so many shells that the car almost dragged on the ground. I collected over fifty sand dollars and thirty-two conch shells. Tomorrow, I'm going to clean them and sort them. My mom says they make my room smell like dead fish.

    At the beach, we ate dinner at the Crab Shack. They had a shell from a crab that was three feet across! My mom and dad ate crab, but I got to eat the biggest corn dog you ever saw. It was almost a foot long. It tasted great, but I felt kind of woozy afterwards.

    I hope you can come to the beach with me next time.

Love from Your Cousin,
Floyd

CONCEPT #7: RESPONDING TO LITERATURE

Foundation Information

When students write a response to literature, they express their thoughts and feelings about what they have read. This activity helps them reach a deeper level of comprehension. It takes a complexity of thought that children aren't capable of until they reach age 8 1/2 or 9.

Students need to be able to read and understand the words on the page and at the same time listen to the messages that their brain is sending them. It's important not to start this activity until the second semester of third grade.

Lesson #58: Responding to Literature--Introduction

Step One: Introduction to Responding to Literature

SCRIPT FOR TEACHERS TO SHARE WITH STUDENTS (or use the video provided online).

Every moment of our lives, our brains are constantly working. Our brains are thinking lots of thoughts about everything we see and hear and smell and taste and feel. Unfortunately, most of those thoughts pass right through our brains and we never really notice them. We are aware of them only as a vague "feeling" or "gut reaction" toward something.

When you were little and just beginning to read, teachers told you to focus on what you were reading. Concentrate on the words. Don't think about other things. This is exactly what they are supposed to tell you when you are learning to read. You have all learned to do it very well, because now you are all great readers.

Now that you can read fluently, you are ready to step up to the next level of reading. You are going to dig deeper and learn to think between the words on the page. You are going to learn to interpret and analyze what is written, why it was written, and how it was written. You're going to learn to read critically and to read between the lines. More importantly, you're going to discover what the words on the page mean to you. In order to do that, you're going to learn to grab hold of some of those thoughts that you learned to ignore while you were little.

Step Two: Introduction to the Response Starters

Display the Response Starters page (p. 127) for the class to see. Use chart paper or your smart board. (Students will need to refer to them in future lessons so make an individual copy for each student.)

Explain to students that these are some examples of things their brains may be thinking about while they are reading or listening to a story.

1. How is this story like another story (either book or television)?

2. How is this character like someone you know?

3. Has something like this happened to you or someone you know?

4. Have you ever felt like the character is feeling?

5. Does the place where this story takes place remind you of a place that is familiar to you?

6. What questions do you ask yourself during the story?

7. This part of the story doesn't seem real.

8. I would or would not like to be the character right now.

9. I really like or dislike the way the author wrote that.

10. How do you feel about the author's choice of setting?

11. Would you have changed anything in the story?

12. I wonder…

Step Three: Guided Practice

Read the book *Alexander and the Terrible, Horrible, No Good, Very Bad Day* by Judith Viorst to the students.

Write the following responses on the board one at a time. Allow students time to decide which of the Response Starters was used to write the response.

Ask for answers and discuss with the class.

1. It's impossible to draw a picture of an invisible castle. (7)

2. My sister stuck gum in the dog's fur and they had to shave a spot on his back. (3)

3. I had a horrible day like Alexander once. (4)

Step Four: Independent Practice

Distribute a copy of the Response Sorting Page (p. 128) to each student.

Divide students into pairs. Complete the first two with students. Then the students will read each response and work with their partner to decide which Response Starter was used.

Allow 15-20 minutes or until most pairs are finished. Review the answers with the class. Ask students to justify their answers.

Lesson #59: Learning to Respond

Step One: Choose the Book

Make sure that the ten response starters from Lesson # 58 are posted in the room.

Choose a picture book that doesn't have too much text. The story should be engaging and have dramatic or thought-provoking pieces of writing and pictures on most pages. Here is a list of books that work well with this activity:

Humphrey's Bear   by Jan Wahl and William Joyce
Beardream   by Will Hobbs
Pigsty   by Mark Teague

Step Two: Modeling the Response to Literature

Ask students to picture ideas going over their heads as if they were flowing in a stream. They should reach up over their heads and pretend to grab onto those ideas, catch them, and put them on their paper. This mindset is important. The more they buy into this, the easier this process will be.

Distribute a sheet of paper to each student and make sure they have a pencil ready.

Read the first page of the book to them. Then the teacher should talk about their own personal responses to the text and the picture. Record those responses on the chalkboard, overhead projector, or smart board to show students how to record their responses.

A teacher sample for the first two pages of each of the suggested books is provided on p. 129.

To streamline the recording process, students should:

- Begin each response on new line, even if the line before it is not full.
- Number each new thought or idea.
- Write as many responses for each page as they can.

Read the second page of the book. Again, the teacher should talk about their own personal responses to the page and record them for the students.

Ask students to try to find a response to the next page. Read the third page of the book. Ask them to write down one response to the page. After a few minutes, ask each student to share what they're written. Students get ideas from each other. Often they will realize that they had the same thought as another student, but they didn't quite grab on to it so they could write it down.

When teaching this lesson for the first time, an entire class period may be spent on modeling. On the second repetition of this activity, the amount of time spend modeling can be decreased. During the third exercise, the time can be decreased even farther, or eliminated it altogether, depending on the students' progress.

Step Three: Independent Practice

Students will write their responses as the teacher reads. They should write down every single thought that comes into their head.

Read the page slowly, pausing between sentences. After finishing, give students a few minutes to finish writing. Then reread the page again. Give the students a few more minutes to write.

When most students have finished writing, ask them to share their favorite response.

Read the remainder of the book and allow students to share after each

page. Collect pages.

Step Four: Rough Draft

Read through the ideas that the students have written down. Circle the one (or possibly two) that will be the easiest for the child to write about.

Once in a while, there will be a student that did not write down anything that can be used as a topic for further writing. Pull that student aside and ask them to look at the book again and orally tell about their reactions to one or two of their favorite pages. A suitable topic will usually emerge.

During the second repetition of this lesson, students should be asked to circle the three they would most like to write about. Then collect the papers and read all the choices, not just the circled ones. If any of the circled choices are a good choice, put a check mark by them. However, sometimes students choose topics that are just too difficult for them and it's up to the teacher to choose one or more that they did not circle.

Return the papers to the students and distribute clean pieces of writing paper. Ask students to copy their chosen topic onto the paper.

Students should then write only about this item. Remind them that this is a rough draft. Students should write their ideas as they occur and not worry at this time about spelling or making sure that all the ideas fit together. They should be able to fill the front side of a standard sheet of paper.

Step Five: Revise for Focus and Edit

Follow the standard directions for revising for focus (p. 130) and editing student work. (p. 132)

Step Six: Title the work. See p. 133.

Step Seven: Publish

Follow the standard directions for publishing student work. (p. 133)

Step Eight: Presentation

Follow the standard directions for presentations. (p. 135)

Response Starters

1. How is this story like another story (either book or television)?

2. How is this character like someone you know?

3. Has something like this happened to you or someone you know?

4. Have you ever felt like the character is feeling?

5. Does the place where this story takes place remind you of a place that is familiar to you?

6. What questions do you ask yourself during the story?

7. This part of the story doesn't seem real.

8. I would or would not like to be the character right now.

9. I really like or dislike the way the author wrote that.

10. How do you feel about the author's choice of setting?

11. Would you have changed anything in the story?

12. I wonder…

Response Sort Page

Name_____

1._____ I always had to ride in the back seat like Alexander and I always got carsick.

2._____The shoe store in the book reminds me of the old shoe store I went to when I was seven.

3._____When Alexander is trying on shoes, it reminds me of the story of *Cinderella*.

4. _____I do not like Alexander. He complains too much. The author should have made him say something happy.

5. _____The dentist looks like my Uncle Frank.

6._____I wonder why there is a plant hanging over Alexander's head at the table.

7._____It's impossible for Alexander to go to Australia.

8._____When Alexander slipped and fell in the mud, it reminded me of the time I fell on the sidewalk at school and broke my tooth.

9._____I would not like to be Alexander when his best friend told him he didn't want to be his friend anymore. That would hurt my feelings.

10._____I think it was funny that Alexander told Paul that he hoped his ice cream would fall off and land in Australia.

11._____When Alexander said he didn't like lima beans, it reminded me of the book, *Gregory the Terrible Eater*.

12._____The bathroom in Alexander's house reminds me of the bathroom in my Grandma's house.

13._____Why does Alexander's father have a bottle of ink on his desk?

14._____Alexander's brother took his pillow back. It was just like when my friend, Amanda, took back the book she gave me.

15._____It doesn't seem real that Alexander would skip 16 when he was counting.

16._____It might have been funnier if the author had chosen a different country each time instead of always saying Australia.

Possible Responses to Literature Books

Humphrey's Bear
Page 1

   1. When Humphrey's father asks if he's too old to sleep with his bear, it reminded me of the time when my mom asked me if I was too old to play with dolls.

   2. Humphrey is hiding in the hall when he's supposed to be in bed. It reminds me of when I used to sneak out of bed to watch TV.

   3. The stairs in Humphrey's house look dark and scary like the ones that led to my Grandma's cellar.

Page 2

   1. Humphrey's pillow is huge.

   2. Humphrey's pillow reminds me of the joke about the boy that dreamed that he ate a 5-pound marshmallow and when he woke up, his pillow was gone.

   3. Does the bear's hat tickle Humphrey when he sleeps?

   4. Sometimes at night when I'm scared, I jump in bed and pull the covers over my head.

   5. I had a toy dinosaur that I snuggled with at night.

Bear Dream
Page 1

   1. Once when I was sick, I slept all day.

   2. My Uncle Jim loves to go fishing in the mountains.

   3. The bear sitting in the pond reminds me of the time my sister fell into the pond in our yard.

   4. I wouldn't like to be that bear. I think that water is too cold.

Page 2

   1. Sometimes my dreams seem like they're real.

   2. My cousin puts flowers in her salad and eats them.

3. I wonder if bears really play in the snow. Do they make snow bears?

4. This bear reminds me of the bear in *Brown Bear, Brown Bear, What Do You See?*.

Pigsty

Page 1

1. I wonder if Wendell wore those ugly shorts to school.

2. His mother looks angry because her hand is on her hip. When my mother gets angry, she waves her hands around.

3. Sometimes my room turns into a pigsty too.

4. Wendell's mother's hair looks like my Aunt Peggy's hair. It was always stiff like she was wearing a wig.

5. It makes me mad when my mom starts telling me to clean my room the minute I come home. I'm tired and hungry and all I want to do is have a snack and watch cartoons.

Page 2

1. I'd be surprised if I found a pig in my bed.

2. I would not want to sleep in my bed after a dirty pig layed on it.

3. I don't think a pig can bend his elbows like that.

4. I like to sleep with the window open like the pig.

5. I wonder how that pig got in there.

6. When Wendell finds the pig in his bed, it reminds me of the story of *Goldilocks and the Three Bears*.

7. Once I went into my room and found my cousin sleeping in my room.

CONCEPT #8: REVISING FOR FOCUS

Composing a focused piece of writing is one of the skills of a talented writer. Sometimes mature, experienced writers can take a topic and write with focus from the first or second sentence onward through an entire piece. For everyone else, finding the focus for a piece of writing is a process of discovery.

During the rough draft phase, make sure that students fill at least one side of a piece of filler paper. Remind them to use similes when they write. Once the rough draft is completed, set them aside for a day or two before returning them. Teach students how to find a focus. (See below.) Ask them to get out a colored pencil or crayon and underline a sentence or idea that will be the focus of their writing. If they find more than one, they should use a different color for each one. Then they should choose only one that they will write about. Teachers should review students' choices.

After students read their papers, some still may not be able to find a focus. Pair these students with another student in the class that is unable to find their focus and ask them to trade papers and

try again. At the end of the process, if they still cannot find their focus, teacher assistance may be needed. Teachers should not feel uncomfortable if they need to point out the focus for students. Students will find this process easier with practice.

Once students have decided on a single focus, they should read through their writing again, underlining all the sentences that talk about their focus.

Distribute a new piece of filler paper to each student. Students are going to write their focus sentence or idea on the new paper. They will then write a new rough draft, writing only about the sentence or idea they chose.

It's recommended that you initially complete this exercise in small groups. The remaining students can be working on independent writing assignments.

Finding a Focus

1. Is there something that is mentioned over and over again? That is probably the focus.

2. Is there a sentence or idea that really grabs your interest? Is there an idea that

is really unusual? That is probably the focus.

If there is no focus to be found, the student must return to the rough draft phase. They should make sure that they are using their five senses in their description. They need to make sure that they are using similes and they need to make sure that they are writing about their feelings. They can either start over from the beginning or they can add to the description that they have already completed.

Eventually, students will be able to identify their focus as they are writing the rough draft and then to continue writing about it until the end of the piece.

It usually happens something like this: The student is writing along and they write a particularly great sentence. They think, "I like this idea! It's cool!" Then they begin to write only about that sentence. It is important for students to understand that this is the goal. Otherwise when this happens, they think they're doing something wrong because they're only writing about one thing.

During this first year of writing, do not emphasize the need to find a focus during the rough draft stage of writing unless you have a particularly skilled writer. It is important that students learn to access and write down all the ideas that occur to them, as they occur, without worrying about whether they fit together or not.

EDITING

The editing phase of writing should occur just before the final draft/ publishing phase.

During this phase, students will be correcting spelling and grammar mistakes. Editing techniques will vary according to students' ability levels.

1. A Few Random Mistakes

If the student is high functioning, then underline all the spelling and grammar mistakes and let the students go through and correct all the mistakes.

2. Repeatedly Misspelling the Same Word

If a student has misspelled the same word many times throughout the piece, write the word correctly at the top of the paper and ask the student to find and correct all occurrences. When they are through, ask the student to spell the word orally.

3. Spelling and Grammar Rule Violations

If a student repeatedly breaks a spelling or grammar rule throughout the piece of writing, underline each

occurrence. Ask the student to state the rule which should have been followed and then ask them to correct the mistake.

Repeat this for each occurrence. Over time, the repetition of the rule will help the student learn it and they will no longer make the same mistake.

4. The Verb Tense is Not Consistent

It is not unusual for students to change the tense of their verbs in a single piece of writing. Ask the student to identify the verb in the first sentence of their writing. Ask them to identify the verb's tense; past, present, or future.

Remind them that all the verbs in a single piece of writing should be the same tense. Ask them to read and identify any verbs that are not in the correct form. Students should then correct them. At first, the teacher may have to underline the incorrect words for them.

CONCEPT #9: PUBLISHING

Students notice when teachers consider things important even when they don't say a word. If a teacher simply passes back their writing with a grade on it, students will believe that their writing is not highly regarded. If a student feels that they are writing for nothing, they lose their incentive to write their best. If a teacher hands back papers full of red marks, students will lose their enthusiasm for writing. The final copies of all student work should be proudly displayed in the classroom.

Make sure that students write the date on their final copy. It helps parents track their child's progress more closely. It also allows the child to see how much they have improved from one piece to another.

Before publishing, be sure to recheck students' work after they have written the final copy. No matter how many times the work has been proof-read, errors seem to sneak into the final copy.

Choosing a Title

Students often want to write the title of their work before they have written it. It can be a difficult task to get students to understand that they can't write a title for something they have not yet written. The title should be written after the final draft is completed.

Do not minimize the importance of writing a title for a piece of writing. This is yet another link between writing and reading comprehension abilities. Student's comprehension is often tested by asking them to read a written passage and identify its main idea.

When students choose a title for their writing, they are actually learning to discern the main idea. Therefore, it is very important to include this step with every writing assignment.

Key Teaching Points:

1. The title should tell the reader what your writing is about.

2. Review all suggestions with each student individually. This only takes a few

minutes. Ask students to reread their writing and when they come up with a possible title, to raise their hand. Then the teacher can review the choice with the child. If it does not seem to reflect the main idea of the writing, point out to the students those parts of the writing which will lead them to a better title.

The more practice that they have, the more skillful they'll become. Once a month, during the time set aside for students to read their writing to the class, ask them not to read the titles right away. Instead, distribute pieces of scratch paper to each student. After a child has read their piece of writing, give the other students time to write down a title. Share the answers. Ask students to explain why they chose that title. Then ask the author to share their title and share the reason for choosing their title.

Presenting five or six pieces of writing in this fashion will take an entire writing period, so spread this activity over several days

Five Ways to Publish Students' Work

1. One easy way to publish students' work is to provide students with writing paper with great borders which the students can color. There are many books available for purchase. Mount the writing on colorful paper and laminate if possible.

2. If students have access to computer presentation software such as Hyperstudio or PowerPoint, student work can be made into a computerized presentation.

3. Longer works can be published in book form. Students can copy their work by hand or type it using a word processing program. A paragraph or scene can be written on each piece of paper and then the page can be illustrated. These pages can then be bound into a book.

4. Another way to publish student work is to mount the final copy on a 12" x 18" piece of construction paper as shown on the following page. If students illustrate their writing on a piece of 8 1/2" x 11" bond paper, it will mount perfectly above the student's writing. Laminate them if possible.

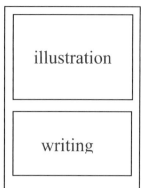

Presentation

Oral language is an important element in the writing process. Like publishing, it provides students with the opportunity to share their writing. If students know that they will read their work aloud, it gives them an extra impetus to write well.

5. In addition to these, teachers can create a yearly magazine containing samples of students' work. Teachers should save the final copy of all students' work. Near the end of the first semester, students should be allowed to choose two or three of their favorite pieces of writing. Those pieces would then be typed using a word processing program. The process would be repeated near the end of the second semester.

Each student would then receive a copy of the magazine during the final week of school. Students are asked to read another student's work and then go to them and ask them to autograph their work.

CONCEPT #10: EVALUATION

The most important thing that teachers expect from a student's writing is improvement. At the start of each practice exercise, it's important to restate the expectation that they write better every time they write. If they're writing a paragraph or a description, ask them to try to remember the things they learned during the last writing assignment and apply it to the current writing assignment.

Rubrics are the easiest way to objectively determine improvement. Included in this section, there are rubrics for a single paragraph, multiple paragraphs, a story, a description, a personal letter, and a response to literature. Use the multiple paragraph rubric to evaluate the compare and contrast paragraphs written using a Venn diagram.

The rubrics are primarily for use as a tool for teachers. However, every teacher knows that it's important for students to understand how they're being evaluated. Always tell students ahead of time that a particular piece of writing is going to be graded.

Lesson # 60 Teaching Students to Evaluate

This lesson should take place about a week before the actual evaluation. It should be repeated before each evaluation. You will need two samples of students' writing with students' names removed. These samples can be used each year.

This lesson is not included on the calendar. Because every class moves at its own pace, teachers should schedule this lesson at their discretion.

Step One: Direct Instruction

Distribute a copy of the appropriate rubric. Read through the rubric with the students. Explain the meaning of each block and show them how the point system words.

Step Two: Guided Practice

Make copies of one of the student samples and distribute a copy to each student. Read the sample out loud with students.

Begin with the first item on the rubric. Ask students to reread the sample silently and decide how many points it should earn. Students may write the points on the student sample. Ask for volunteers to tell how many points they awarded. Ask them to explain why they awarded that number of points. Then the teacher should tell the number of points that they would award and explain why.

Repeat this process with the remaining items on the rubric.

Then add the points and show students the grade that this paper earned.

Step Three: Independent Practice

Distribute copies of the second student writing sample. On a piece of paper, students will write down the score for each section of the rubric. They should then write a sentence explaining why they gave that score.

They should add all the points and give a grade for the writing sample.

When they are finished, the students should share their results.

The teacher will then tell students how they would score each section of the rubric.

Single Paragraph Rubric

	5 Points	4 Points	3 Points	1 Point
Organization	The paragraph started with a topic sentence and used supporting details.	The paragraph started with a topic sentence but only some of the detail sentences supported it.	The paragraph started with a topic sentence but the detail sentences did not support it.	No topic sentence
Sentence fluency	Sentences are varied in length and type.	Some sentences vary in length and type.	Sentences have little variety.	Sentences have no variety.
Writing Conventions	No Mistakes	2-3 errors	4-5 errors	Consistent errors
Sentence Structure	Complete Sentences—no fragments or run-on sentences.	Less than 2 fragments or run-on sentences.	Less than 2 fragments or run-on sentences.	Most sentences are incomplete or run-on sentences.

Score: 18-20 points, Grade: A
Score: 14- 17 points, Grade B
Score: 9-13 points, Grade C
Score: 4-8 points, Grade D

Multiple Paragraph Rubric

	5 Points	4 Points	3 Points	1 Point
Organization	There are 2 or more paragraphs and each starts with a topic sentence. The details in all the paragraphs support the topic sentences.	There are 2 or more paragraphs and each starts with a topic sentence. Some of the details in the paragraphs support the topic sentences.	There is only one paragraph and it started with a topic sentence. The details supported the topic sentence.	There is only one paragraph and there was no topic sentence.
Sentence fluency	Sentences are varied in length and type.	Some sentences vary in length and type.	Sentences have little variety.	Sentences have no variety.
Writing Conventions	No Mistakes	3-5 errors	6-8 errors	Consistent errors
Sentence Structure	Complete Sentences—no fragments or run-on sentences.	Less than 2 fragments or run-on sentences.	Less than 4 fragments or run-on sentences.	Most sentences are incomplete or run-on sentences.

Score: 18-20 points, Grade: A
Score: 14- 17 points, Grade B
Score: 9-13 points, Grade C
Score: 4-8 points, Grade D

Letter Writing Rubric

	5 Points	4 Points	3 points	1 Point
Return Address	The return address has all of the parts and no punctuation errors.	The return address has all of the parts and 1-2 punctuation errors.	The return address is missing one part and has one or less punctuation errors.	The return address is missing more than one part or has more than two punctuation errors.
Greeting	The greeting is included and has no punctuation errors.	There is a comma after the greeting, but there is a capitalization mistake.	There is no comma after the greeting.	There is no greeting.
Body	The body of the letter includes details and has correct punctuation.	The body of the letter includes details and has less than three punctuation errors. It is indented.	The body of the letter includes few details or is not indented.	The body of the letter is not indented. It also has four or more punctuation errors or no details.
Closing and Signature	Closing and signature are punctuated correctly.	There is no comma after the closing or the closing and signature are on the same line.	There is no comma after the closing and the closing and signature are on the same line.	Closing or signature is missing.

Score: 18-20 points, Grade: A
Score: 14- 17 points, Grade B
Score: 9-13 points, Grade C
Score: 4-8 points, Grade D

Descriptive Writing Rubric

	5 Points	4 Points	3 Points	1 Point
Descriptive Details	Many sensory sentences and similes.	Few sensory sentences and similes.	Sensory details but no similes.	No sensory details.
Sentence Fluency	Sentences are varied in length and type.	Most sentences vary in length and type.	A few sentences vary in length and type.	Sentences have no variety.
Focus	The paragraph focuses on a single idea.	Most of the sentences are focused on one idea, but a few sentences are about other ideas.	A few sentences are focused on one idea, but most sentences are about other ideas.	The paragraph contains many different ideas.
Writing Conventions	No Mistakes	3-4 errors	5-7 errors	Consistent errors
Sentence Structure	Complete Sentences—no fragments or run-on sentences.	Less than 2 fragments or run-on sentences.	Less than 4 fragments or run-on sentences.	Most sentences are incomplete or run-on sentences.

Score: 18-20 points, Grade: A
Score: 14- 17 points, Grade B
Score: 9-13 points, Grade C
Score: 4-8 points, Grade D

Response to Literature Rubric

	5 Points	4 Points	3 points	1 Point
Organization	There is a detailed response and there is a clear comparison to part of the story.	The response is detailed, but there is no comparison to part of the story.	The response is not detailed but there is a comparison to part of the story.	The response is not detailed and there is a comparison to part of the story.
Focus	The paragraph focuses on a single part of the story and includes lots of details.	The paragraph focuses on a single part of the story, but doesn't include enough details.	The paragraph includes responses to several parts of the story.	The paragraph is a list of facts from the story.
Writing Conventions	No Mistakes	3 errors or less	4-5 errors	Consistent errors
Sentence Structure	Complete Sentences—no fragments or run-on sentences.	Less than 2 fragments or run-on sentences.	3-4 fragments or run-on sentences.	Most sentences are incomplete or run-on sentences.

Score: 18-20 points, Grade: A
Score: 14- 17 points, Grade B
Score: 9-13 points, Grade C
Score: 4-8 points, Grade D

Story Writing Rubric

	5 Points	4 Points	3 Points	1 Point
Organization	The problem and solution are clearly shown. The story has at least 2 plot points.	The problem and solution are clearly shown. The story has less than 2 plot points.	The problem or the solution is missing or unclear.	There is no clear problem and solution.
The Setting	There is a description of the setting in every scene. The scenes have many sensory details.	There is a description of the setting in every scene. The scenes have some sensory details.	There is a description of the setting in most scenes. There are few sensory details.	Most scenes don't contain a description of the setting.
The Action	Every step of the action in each scene is described in detail.	Some of the action in each scene is described in detail.	Some of the action in some of the scenes is described in detail.	The action is told in only two or three sentences.
Writing Conventions	No more than one mistake in each scene.	No more than three mistakes in each scene.	No more than five mistakes in each scene.	Consistent errors
Sentence Structure	Complete Sentences—no fragments or run-on sentences.	Less than two fragments or run-on sentences.	Less than five fragments or run-on sentences.	Most sentences are incomplete or run-on sentences.

Score 23-25 points, Grade: A
Score 20-22 points, Grade: B
Score 15-19 points, Grade: C
Score 5-14 points, Grade: D

CONCEPT #11: INDEPENDENT WRITING

Although this book's focus is on guided writing, it's important to address independent writing briefly as well. The two items are indelibly linked. During independent writing time, students practice the skills they learned during guided writing.

Time for Independent Writing

Both independent writing and guided writing should be done every day. Independent writing can be done during the time that the teacher is working with small groups on a guided writing assignment. It can also be assigned during reading group time if you do stations or learning centers.

During independent writing time, students should be encouraged to stretch their writing muscles and enjoy writing.

Topics for Independent Writing

As soon as students have achieved independence in a writing skill, it can become part of your repertoire for independent writing. If you can incorporate topics from your social studies or science unit or the story your class is reading in your classroom reading anthology, then you actually get double practice with one assignment. It will reinforce the content concept as well as providing writing skills practice.

There are several books that contain excellent suggestions for writing prompts for independent writing. You can find these and all the other books referenced in this book at our website: www.WritingandKids.com.

Managing Independent Writing

Independent writing should begin after the first guided writing lessons are complete—usually about the fourth week of school. Small composition books with 40 pages seem to work well. As a general rule, most assignments should be about ½ page long.

To help the students stay organized, teach them to write with this format: Write today's date, write the assignment, skip a line, repeat. They should write continuously through the notebook, starting the next assignment right after finishing the last one. They should write on both sides of the paper.

Evaluating Independent Writing

It's easy to check each student's independent writing each day as you check their homework. You don't need to spend no more than 30 seconds per child. It's not necessary to actually read them.

Check to make sure it's written in proper paragraph format: properly indented with a topic sentence. If it isn't, write a paragraph symbol where the indentation should be, write "topic sentence" where the topic sentence should be.

Check to make sure the assignment is at least half a page long. If not, I, "too short" if it's too short.

Write "not done" if they made no attempt at the assignment.

Collect the books every four-five weeks. At that time, read the assignments and give a single independent writing grade, based on effort and improvement.

1. Lesson #10 Story Writing-- Find out what they know p.27	2. Lesson #1 Fiction and Non- fiction p.10	3. Lesson #2 Fiction and Non- fiction Card Game p.10	4. Lesson #3 Characteristics of Fiction and Non- fiction p.40	5. Lesson #18 Introduce the Setting p.40
6. Lesson #19 Describing the Setting Guided Practice p.42	7. Lesson #20 Describing the Setting Practice Level 1 p.42	8. Lesson #21 Describing the Setting Practice Level 2 p.43	9. Lesson #22 Describing the Setting Practice Level 3 p.44	10. Lesson #2 Remediate using the Fiction and Non- fiction card game p.10
11. Lesson #6 Introduction to Similes p.20	12. Lesson #6 Introduction to Similes p.20	13. Lesson #8 Similes Practice Level 2 p.21	14. Lesson #9 Similes Practice Level 3 Steps 1 & 2 p.22	15. Lesson #9 Similes Practice Level 3 Step 3 p.22
16. Lesson #2 Remediate using the Fiction and Non- fiction card game p.10	17. Lesson #23 Describing the Setting Practice Level 4 Steps 1, 2, & 3 p.45	18. Lesson #23 Describing the Setting Practice Level 4 Step 4 p.47	19. Lesson #23 Describing the Setting Practice Level 4 Step 4 p.47	20. Lesson #24 Revising the Sentence Structure p.47
21. Lesson #23 Describing the Setting Practice Level 4 Step 5 p.47	22. Lesson #23 Describing the Setting Practice Level 4 Step 6 p.47	23. Lesson #23 Describing the Setting Practice Level 4 Step 6 p.47	24. Lesson #23 Describing the Setting Practice Level 4 Step 7,8,9,10 p.47	25. Lesson #23 Describing the Setting Practice Level 4 Step 7,8,9,10 p.47

26. Lesson #34 Introduction to Paragraph Writing p.71	27. Lesson #35 Paragraph Webs Steps 1, 2, & 3 "Starfish" p.72	28. Lesson #35 Paragraph Webs Step 4 "Crabs" p.74	29. Lesson #35 Paragraph Webs Steps 4 "Crabs" p.74	30. Lesson #36 Continuing Paragraph Web Practice "Octopuses" p.75
31. Remediation day for students that need to revise their Starfish, Crabs, or Octopus paragraphs	32. Lesson #36 Continuing Paragraph Web Practice "Jellyfish" p.75	33. Lesson #36 Continuing Paragraph Web Practice "Sea Anemones" p.75	34. Lesson #36 Continuing Paragraph Web Practice Remediation Day p. 75	35. Lesson #36 Continuing Paragraph Web Practice "Sharks" p. 75
36. Lesson #36 Continuing Paragraph Web Practice "Shrimp" p.75	37. Lesson #36 Continuing Paragraph Web Practice Remediation Day p.77	38. Lesson #39 Topic Sentence Practice p.78	39. Lesson #40 More Topic Sentence Practice p.78	40. Lesson #41 Writing Paragraphs from Prompts p.78
41. Lesson #51 Venn Diagram-- Direct Instruction p. 110	42. Lesson #51 Venn Diagram-- Direct Instruction p. 110	43. Lesson #52 Venn Diagram-- Practice Level 1 p. 112	44. Lesson #52 Venn Diagram-- Practice Level 1 p. 112	45. Lesson #53 Venn Diagram-- Practice Level 2 p. 113
46. Lesson #53 Venn Diagram-- Practice Level 2 p. 113	47. Lesson #53 Venn Diagram-- Practice Level 2 p. 113	48. Lesson #25 Describing the Setting Practice Level 5 Steps 1,2 p.48	49. Lesson #25 Describing the Setting Practice Level 5 Step 3,4,5 p.48	50. Lesson #25 Describing the Setting Practice Level 5 Step 3,4,5 p.48

51. Lesson #25 Describing the Setting Practice Level 5 Step 3,4,5 p.48	56. Lesson #28 Character Profile-- Introduction p.60	61. Lesson #32 Problem and Solution-- Independent Practice Step 5 p.67	66. Lesson #13 Write a Story-- Rough Draft p.32	71. Lesson #13 Write a Story-- Rough Draft p.32
52. Lesson #25 Describing the Setting Practice Level 5 Step 6,7,8,9 p.48	57. Lesson #29 Character Profile-- Guided Practice p.61	62. Lesson #33 Introduction to the Plot p.29	67. Lesson #13 Write a Story-- Rough Draft p.32	72. Lesson #14 Revise the Story p.33
53. Lesson #25 Describing the Setting Practice Level 5 Step 6,7,8,9 p.48	58. Lesson #30 Character Profile-- Independent Practice p.62	63. Lesson #11 Plan the Story p.29	68. Lesson #13 Write a Story-- Rough Draft p.32	73. Lesson #14 Revise the Story p.33
54. Lesson #25 Describing the Setting Practice Level 5 Step 6,7,8,9 p.48	59. Lesson #31 Introduction to Problem and Solution p.65	64. Lesson #11 Plan a Story p.29	69. Lesson #13 Write a Story-- Rough Draft p.32	74. Lesson #15 Edit the Story p.34
55. Lesson #25 Describing the Setting Practice Level 5 Step 6,7,8,9 p.48	60. Lesson #32 Problem and Solution-- Independent Practice Steps #1-4 p.66	65. Lesson #12 Scene Building p.30	70. Lesson #13 Write a Story-- Rough Draft p.32	75. Lesson #15 Edit the Story p.34

76.	Lesson #16	Write a Story-- Final Copy	p.34
77.	Lesson #16	Write a Story-- Final Copy	p.34
78.	Lesson #17	Write a Story-- Choosing the Title	p.34
79.	Lesson #42	Web to Paragraph Review	p.93
80.	Lesson #43	Paragraph to Web Direct Instruction and Guided Practice	p.93
81.	Lesson #44	Paragraph to Web-- Independent Practice	p.94
82.	Lesson #45	Introduction to Multiple Paragraph Web Patterns Level 2	p.98
83.	Lesson #46	Multiple Paragraph Web Patterns Level 3	p.99
84.	Lesson #47	Multiple Paragraph Web Patterns Level 3	p.99
85.	Lesson #48	Multiple Paragraph Web Practice Level 1	p.100
86.	Lesson #48	Multiple Paragraph Web Practice Level 1	p.100
87.	Lesson #48	Multiple Paragraph Web Practice Level 1	p.100
88.	Lesson #48	Multiple Paragraph Web Practice Level 1	p.100
89.	Remediation Day		
90.	**2nd Semester** Lesson #58	Responding to Literature-- Introduction	p.122
91.	Lesson #59	Learning to Respond Steps #1, 2, 3	p.124
92.	Lesson #59	Learning to Respond Step #4	p.125
93.	Lesson #59	Learning to Respond Step #5, 6, 7	p.126
94.	Lesson #59	Learning to Respond Step #5, 6, 7	p.126
95.	Lesson #59	Learning to Respond Step #5, 6, 7	p.126
96.	Lesson #59	Learning to Respond Step #5, 6, 7	p.126
97.	Lesson #59	Learning to Respond Step #8	p.126
98.	Lesson #49	Multiple Paragraph Web Practice Level 2	p.101
99.	Lesson #49	Multiple Paragraph Web Practice Level 2	p.101
100.	Lesson #49	Multiple Paragraph Web Practice Level 2	p.101

101. Lesson #49 Multiple Paragraph Web Practice Level 2 p.101	106. Lesson #54 Venn Diagram--Practice Level 3 p.113	111. Lesson #59 Learning to Respond Step #5, 6, 7 p.126	116. Lesson #2 Review Fiction and Non-fiction using the card game p.10	121. Lesson #5 Object Description Steps 3 & 4 p.19
102. Lesson #55 Letter Writing--the Return Address p.116	107. Lesson #54 Venn Diagram--Practice Level 3 p.113	112. Lesson #59 Learning to Respond Step #5, 6, 7 p.126	117. Lesson #4 Object Description Introduction p.17	122. Lesson #5 Object Description Steps 5, 6, 7, 8, & 9 p.19
103. Lesson #56 Introduction to Letter Writing p.116	108. Lesson #54 Venn Diagram--Practice Level 3 p.113	113. Lesson #59 Learning to Respond Step #5, 6, 7 p.126	118. Lesson #5 Object Description Steps 1 & 2 p.18	123. Lesson #5 Object Description Steps 5, 6, 7, 8, & 9 p.19
104. Lesson #56 Introduction to Letter Writing p.116	109. Lesson #59 Learning to Respond Steps #1, 2, 3 p.124	114. Lesson #59 Learning to Respond Step #5, 6, 7 p.126	119. Lesson #5 Object Description Steps 1 & 2 p.18	124. Lesson #5 Object Description Steps 5, 6, 7, 8, & 9 p.19
105. Lesson #57 Letter Writing Practice Level 2 p.117	110. Lesson #59 Learning to Respond Step #4 p.125	115. Lesson #59 Learning to Respond Step #8 p.125	120. Lesson #5 Object Description Steps 3 & 4 p.19	125. Lesson #5 Object Description Steps 5, 6, 7, 8, & 9 p.19

126. Lesson #11 Plan a Story p.29	127. Lesson #11 Plan a Story p.29	128. Lesson #13 Write a Story-- Rough Draft p.32	129. Lesson #13 Write a Story-- Rough Draft p.32	130. Lesson #13 Write a Story-- Rough Draft p.32
131. Lesson #13 Write a Story-- Rough Draft p.32	132. Lesson #14 Revise the Story p.33	133. Lesson #14 Revise the Story p.33	134. Lesson #15 Edit the Story p.34	135. Lesson #15 Edit the Story p.34
136. Lesson #16 Write a Story-- Final Copy p.34	137. Lesson #17 Write a Story-- Choosing the Title p.34	138. Lesson #27 Cross-Curricular Setting Steps 1 & 2 p.50	139. Lesson #27 Cross-Curricular Setting Step 3 p.51	140. Lesson #27 Cross-Curricular Setting Step 3 p.51
141. Lesson #27 Cross-Curricular Setting Step 3 p.51	142. Lesson #27 Cross-Curricular Setting Steps 4,5,6 p.51	143. Lesson #27 Cross-Curricular Setting Steps 4,5,6 p.51	144. Lesson #27 Cross-Curricular Setting Steps 7,8,9 p.51	145. Lesson #54 Venn Diagram-- Practice Level 3 p.113
146. Lesson #54 Venn Diagram-- Practice Level 3 p.113	147. Lesson #54 Venn Diagram-- Practice Level 3 p.113	148. Lesson #59 Learning to Respond Steps 1,2, & 3 p.124	149. Lesson #59 Learning to Respond Step 4 p.125	150. Lesson #59 Learning to Respond Step 5, 6, 7, & 8 p.126

Answer Key p.13   Introduction to Fiction and Non-Fiction #1

A. Directions: Write each item from the right under the correct title on the left.

FICTION

1. not real

2.   read from beginning to end

3.   read for enjoyment

NON-FICTION

1.   real

2.   read in any direction

3.   read to get information

- Real
- Read from beginning to end
- Read for enjoyment
- Not real
- Read in any direction
- Read to get information

B. Directions: Read the following book titles and answer the questions below.

The title of a book is The Monkey's First Day of School.

1. Is this book fiction or non- fiction?   fiction

2. How do you know?   not real

3. Why is it important to know this? so you know how to read it

The title of a book is The Big Book of Birds.

4. Is this book fiction or non-fiction?   non-fiction

5. How do you know?   real

6. Why is it important to know this?   so you know how to read this

C. Directions: Answer the following questions by writing "fiction" or "non-fiction" on the line.

7. Tracy is reading chapter 5 of her book first and then she will read chapter 8. Is her book fiction or non-fiction?   non-fiction

8. Matthew is spending his Saturday afternoon reading The Pirate's Gold. Is his book fiction or non-fiction?   fiction

9. Marissa needed to find out how much the Liberty Bell weighed so she looked in the book called The Beginning of the United States. Is her book fiction or non-fiction?   non-fiction

10. Jason is reading How to Win Every Video Game Ever Made. Is his book fiction or non-fiction?   non-fiction

Answer Key p.14   Fiction and Non-Fiction Practice #2

Name _____

A. Directions: Write fiction or non-fiction after each of these titles.

1. All About Birds   non-fiction

2. Mrs. Mouse's Song   fiction

3. Jerry's Vacation non-fiction

4. Ghosts in the Closet   fiction

5. Moon Rocks non-fiction

6. Alligators non-fiction

7. Flying Pigs   fiction

8. Monsters in my Desk   fiction

9. Cake Recipes non-fiction

10. Singing Raccoons   fiction

B. Directions: Write the titles of three fiction books. Don't forget to underline the important words in the title.

11. _____Answers will vary_____

12. _____

13. _____

Name three reasons why these books are fiction.

14. ____not real_____

15. ____read from beginning to end_____

16. ____read for enjoyment_____

C. Directions: Write the titles of three non-fiction books. Don't forget to underline the important words in the title.

17. _____Answers will vary_____

18. _____

19. _____

Tell three reasons why these books are non-fiction.

20. ____real_____

21. ____read in any direction_____

22. _____read to get information_____

Answer Key p.54   Revising the Sentence Structure

Rewrite these sentences so that they are a single sentence that doesn't start with the word "I".

1. I heard a song playing on the radio. It sounded like monkeys howling.

The song playing on the radio sounded like monkeys howling.

2. I smelled the cookie. It smelled like an old drain.

The cookie smelled like an old drain.

3. I saw the cat's eyes. They shone like emeralds in the sunlight.

The cat's eyes shone like emeralds in the sunlight.

4. I heard the cola sizzle. It reminded me of fireworks.

The sizzle of the cola reminds me of fireworks.

5. I tasted the wind. It was fresh and clean like clean towels.

The wind tasted fresh and clean like clean towels.

6. I saw the bricks. They were stacked like a baby's building blocks.

The bricks were stacked like a baby's building blocks.

7. I saw the toys on the floor. They were scattered like rocks by the river.

The toys on the floor were scattered like rocks by the river.

8. I touched the tree's bark. It felt rough like an alligator's skin.

The tree's bark felt rough like an alligator's skin.

9. I smelled the newly sharpened pencils. They reminded me of the first day of school.

The smell of the newly sharpened pencils reminded me of the first day of school.

10. I touched the wet sponge. It felt like raw hamburger.

The wet sponge felt like raw hamburger.

11. I heard the wet shoes plop on the floor. They sounded like the banging of drums.

The wet shoes plopping on the floor sounded like the banging of drums.

12. I heard the children yelling. They were as loud as a rock music band.

The children's yelling was as loud as a rock music band.

13. I stared at the snail's shiny trail. It was silver like a tiny river.

The snail's shiny trail was silver like a tiny river.

Answer Key p. 91   Topic Sentence Worksheet #1

A. Directions: Underline the topic sentence in each paragraph below. Remember that the topic sentence must talk about all of the other sentences in the paragraph.

1.The crust is nice and chewy. <u>Pizza is the best food.</u> Two slices will make you full. The cheese melts in your mouth. You can make it with lots of different things on top.	2. Mix flour and eggs in a big mixing bowl. Stir in sugar and baking powder. Put twelve spoonfuls on a cookie pan and put them in the oven. <u>Making cookies is easy.</u>
3. <u>Raptors are birds that hunt prey.</u> They have good eyes that help them see small animals from far away. Raptors have sharp talons and hooked beaks that help them tear meat. Raptors fly fast to catch prey that is running.	4. There are more kinds of reptiles in the Amazon Jungle than anywhere else. <u>Many animals live in the jungle.</u> Parrots and hummingbirds fly in the jungle. Piranha and catfish swim in the rivers. There are many, many different kinds of ants.

B. **Directions:** In the following paragraphs, cross out the sentence that does not belong.

5. Deserts are very hot. It can be 120 degrees in the daytime. If you walk on the hot ground, you can burn your feet. You will sweat and the sun can burn your skin. ~~Cacti grow in the desert.~~	6. Farmers grow many things on their farms. ~~They have to get up very early in the morning.~~ They raise animals like cows, horses, chickens, and pigs. Some farmers also grow corn, wheat, potatoes, and cotton. They also grow many kinds of fruit like peaches, apples, pears, and apricots.
7. Spiders are the only animals that can spin webs. ~~Spiders have eight eyes.~~ They have special spinnerets on their body that make the silk. They use the webs to catch their food. Spider webs are stronger than steel.	8. We use the roots of many plants for food. Carrots, beets, and sweet potatoes are actually the roots of the plant. Root plants are very good for you. ~~Long ago, people used roots to dye their clothes different colors.~~ Roots contain starch that gives you energy when you eat it.

Answer Key p. 92   Topic Sentence Worksheet #2

A. Directions: Underline the topic sentence in each paragraph below. Remember that the topic sentence must talk about all of the other sentences in the paragraph.

1. North America and South America are two continents. <u>The Earth has seven continents.</u> Australia is the only continent that is an island. Antarctica is a continent that is at the South Pole. The continents of Europe and Asia are right next to each other. The Sahara Desert is found on the continent of Africa.	2. <u>Raisins are made from grapes.</u> The grapes are picked when they are ripe and sweet. Most raisins are made from green grapes. The grapes are placed on paper in the vineyard so the sun can dry them. When they dry, they turn black and wrinkly.
3. You must have a fishing pole to catch a fish. You don't need a boat. Put some bait on your hook and throw it in the water. Reel the fish in when it bites. <u>It is easy to catch a fish.</u>	4. The leaves turn orange, red, yellow, and brown. Some people travel a long way to see the trees changing colors. The trees are shutting down the food making factories in their leaves. <u>The leaves of some trees change color in autumn.</u> The trees are getting ready to rest during the winter.

B. Directions: In the following paragraphs, cross out the sentence that does not belong.

5. Pumpkins come in many sizes. They usually weigh between nine and eighteen pounds. ~~Pumpkins are a kind of squash.~~ Some pumpkins weigh less than a pound. The largest pumpkin recorded weighed an unbelievable 1,810 pounds.	6. There are many ways to eat potatoes. French fries are sliced potatoes that are fried in oil. ~~Potatoes are delicious.~~ Potatoes can be mashed or baked. They can be sliced and cooked with cheese. They can be sliced really thin and made into potato chips.
6. Christopher Columbus sailed to America in 1492. He sailed with three ships named the Nina, the Pinta, and the Santa Maria. It took Christopher Columbus 70 days to reach America. ~~Christopher Columbus had two sons named Diego and Fernando.~~ The trip was paid for by Queen Isabella of Portugal.	7. Milk is good for you. ~~It comes with chocolate and strawberry flavor.~~ It contains protein which helps keep your muscles and other parts of your body healthy. The calcium in milk helps your bones and teeth grow strong. The vitamins in milk keep you from getting sick.

Answer Key p. 103   Multiple Paragraph Web Practice #1
Directions: Draw a web that shows the paragraphs described at the bottom of each box. Write "topic sentence" and "detail sentence" only in your bubbles. In each box, outline each paragraph's bubbles with a different color.

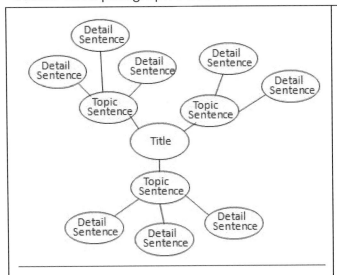

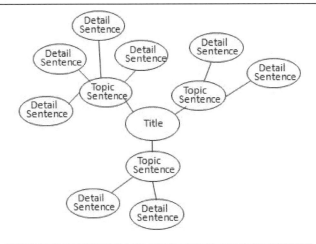

3 paragraphs
1 paragraph with two detail sentences
2 paragraphs with three detail sentences

3 paragraphs
2 paragraphs with two detail sentences
1 paragraph with four detail sentences

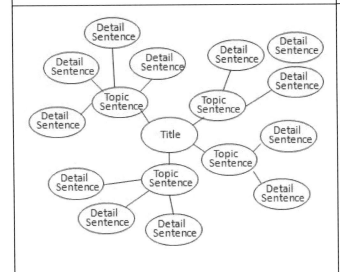

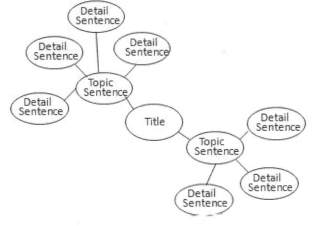

4 paragraphs
1 paragraph with 2 detail sentences
2 paragraphs with 3 detail sentences
1 paragraph with 4 detail sentences

2 paragraphs
1 paragraph with 3 detail sentences
1 paragraph with 4 detail sentences

Multiple Paragraph Web Practice #2

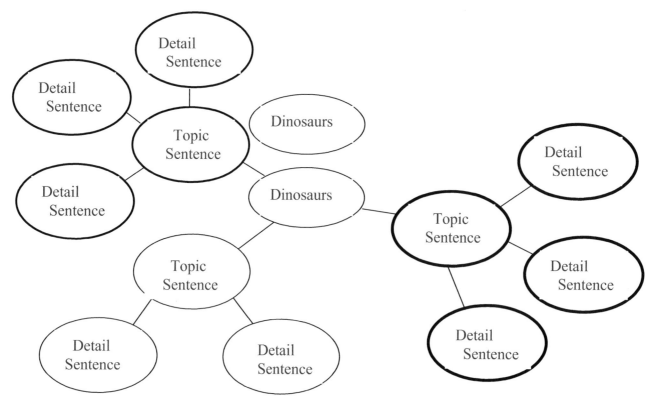

1. How many paragraphs are shown above? __3__

2. How do you know? ____I counted the topic sentences.____

3. How many paragraphs have three detail sentences? ____2____
4. What is the title of these paragraphs? ____Dinosaurs____
5. Outline the bubbles above. Use a different color for each paragraph.
6. In the space below, draw a web showing two paragraphs about spiders. One paragraph will have three detail sentences and one paragraph will have four detail sentences. Write the words "topic sentence" and "detail sentence" and the title only in the bubbles.

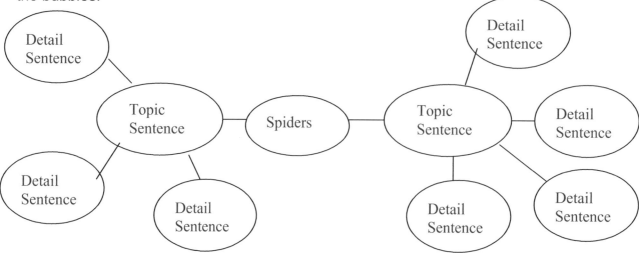

Answer Key p. 105   Multiple Paragraph Web Practice #3
Directions: Draw a web that shows the paragraphs described at the bottom of each
box. Write "topic sentence" and "detail sentence" only in your bubbles. In each box,
outline each paragraph's bubbles with a different color.

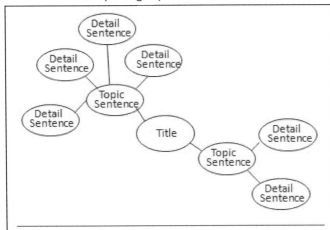

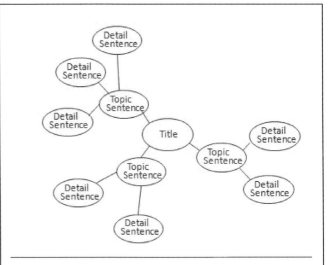

2 paragraphs
1 paragraph with four detail sentences
1 paragraph with two detail sentences

3 paragraphs
2 paragraphs with 2 detail sentences
1 paragraph with 3 detail sentences

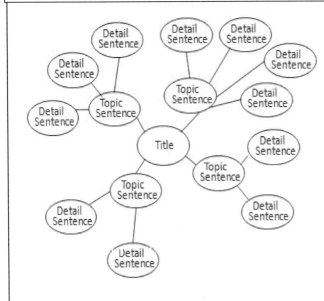

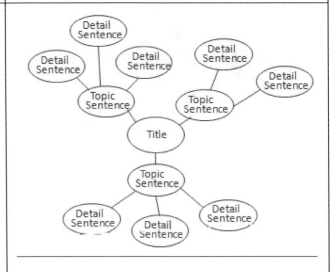

4 paragraphs
1 paragraph with 3 detail sentences
2 paragraphs with 2 detail sentences
1 paragraph with 4 detail sentences

3 paragraphs
2 paragraphs with 3 detail sentences
1 paragraph with 2 detail sentences

Answer Key p. 106   Multiple Paragraph Web Practice #4

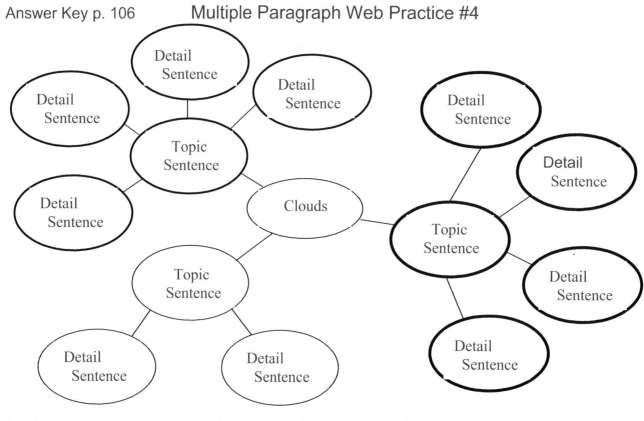

1. How many paragraphs are shown above? _____3_____
2. How do you know? _____I counted the topic sentences._____
_____
3. How many paragraphs have two detail sentences? _____1_____
4. What is the title of these paragraphs? _____Clouds_____
5. Outline the bubbles above. Use a different color for each paragraph.
6. In the space below, draw a web showing three paragraphs about roses. Two paragraphs will have two detail sentences and one paragraph will have three detail sentences. Write the words "topic sentence" and "detail sentence" and the title only in the bubbles.

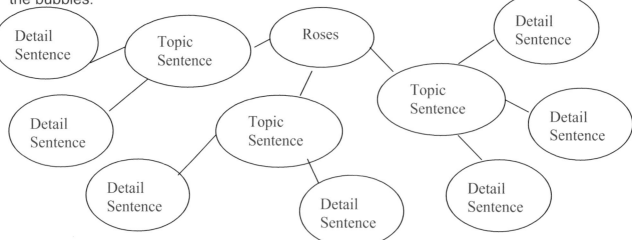

Answer Key p.119   **Return Address**

1.Cindy lives in Memphis, Tennessee (TN), 35701. She lives at 354 Pine Street

354 Pine Street
Memphis, TN 35701
October 4, 2011

2. Gustavo lives at 233 Greentree Ave. in Madera, California (CA), 93637.

233 Greentree Ave.
Madera, CA 93637
October 4, 2011

3. Sophie lives in Phoenix, Arizona (AZ), 85002. She lives at 4909 N. Elm St.

4909 N. Elm St.
Phoenix, AZ 85002
October 4, 2011

4.Jason lives in West Ely, Missouri (MO) 63401 at 56 Smithview Lane.

56 Smithview Lane
West Ely, MO   63401
October 4, 2011

5.Ashley lives in Athens, Georgia (GA) 30609 at 901 E. River Dr.

901 E. River Dr.
Atlanta, GA   30609
October 4, 2011

6.Jeremy lives at 8760 W. Fifth St. in Haverhill, Florida (FL), 33415.

8760 W. Fifth St.
Haverhill, FL   33415
October 4, 2011

7.Hailey lives at 755 Oxford Ave. in Auburn, California (CA),95603.
755 Oxford Ave.
Auburn, CA   95603
October 4, 2011

1. __2__ I always had to ride in the back seat like Alexander and I always got carsick.

2. __5__ The shoe store in the book reminds me of the old shoe store I went to when I was seven.

3. __1__ When Alexander is trying on shoes, it reminds me of the story of *Cinderella*.

4. __11__ I do not like Alexander. He complains too much. The author should have made him say something happy.

5. __2__ The dentist looks like my Uncle Frank.

6. __12__ I wonder why there is a plant hanging over Alexander's head at the table.

7. __7__ It's impossible for Alexander to go to Australia.

8. __3__ When Alexander slipped and fell in the mud, it reminded me of the time I fell on the sidewalk at school and broke my tooth.

9. __8__ I would not like to be Alexander when his best friend told him he didn't want to be his friend anymore. That would hurt my feelings.

10. __9__ I think it was funny that Alexander told Paul that he hoped his ice cream would fall off and land in Australia.

11. __1__ When Alexander said he didn't like lima beans, it reminded me of the book, *Gregory the Terrible Eater*.

12. __5__ The bathroom in Alexander's house reminds me of the bathroom in my Grandma's house.

13. __6__ Why does Alexander's father have a bottle of ink on his desk?

14. __4__ Alexander's brother took his pillow back. It was just like when my friend, Amanda, took back the book she gave me.

15. __7__ It doesn't seem real that Alexander would skip 16 when he was counting.

16. __11__ It might have been funnier if the author had chosen a different country each time instead of always saying Australia.

Order Form

Product	Price	X Quantity	=Total Price
Writing is Exciting! Grade 3	$19.95		
Writing is Exciting! Grade 4	$19.95		
Writing is Exciting! Grade 5	$19.95		
Writing is Exciting! Grade 6	$19.95		
Pre-Writing: More than Just Writing Prompts	$ 8.95		
Shipping and handling	$3 X total number of items		
Total	XXXX		

Payment Method (Sorry, no checks.)

Visa_____   Mastercard_____

Name as shown on card _____

Card #_____

Security #_____ (3-digit number on the back of your card)

Expiration date: Month_____ Year_____

Name _____

Address_____

Email _____

___I would like to receive email about new products.   I teach _____.

Mail this order form to 1105 N. Chapel Hill Ave. Clovis, CA 93611.

You can order these and other products online at www.WritingandKids.com. Many products are available for instant download as digital books.

Visit the other websites in the **Far Journeys Books Publishing Family**. We're dedicated to helping you make life's journey easier, more prosperous, and more fun!

Learn to Write, Publish and Sell your Novel!	If you've ever dreamt of writing a novel, you can follow these easy step by step instructions. You can even get help from the writing coach. Join the Novel Writing Academy at www.NovelWritingAcademy.com.

Do you want to make extra money in your free time?	Do you want to buy a new car or house? Save more money for retirement? Go on a nice vacation? If you need a little extra money, I'll show you a simple way to make money online. Follow these easy step by step instructions and start making money within a week or two. You don't have to be a computer whiz to do this. Join now and get three free ebooks. Visit the Easy Biz Training Center at www.EasyBizOnlineMoney.com.

Find out the secret to true Financial Success!	My husband and I were always working so hard and yet it always seemed like we were barely getting ahead. What was the key to being financially successful? We read books. We went to seminar after seminar. No one seemed to be able to tell us. We invested in mutual funds, a Roth IRA, and real estate. We saved vigorously. It seemed like we were just randomly trying everything that anybody suggested without any real plan.

Then, in 2009, we figured IT out. We knew what the formula was for getting ahead! We wish we'd figured it out earlier, but now we're training our children and grandchildren. Find out the secret to becoming financially independent at www.MoneyHelpPlan.com.

7683563R10091

Made in the USA
San Bernardino, CA
17 January 2014